Camp Michigan's UNOFFICIAL State Park Handbook

Northern Lower Peninsula

IF YOU SEEK A PLEASANT PENINSULA
Camp Michigan
Est. 2018
www.CampMichigan.org

⬥ETAOIN PUBLISHING⬥
www.etaoinpublishing.com

Publisher: Etaoin Publishing
              Saginaw, MI
              www.EtaoinPublishing.com

Ordering Information:
Books may be ordered from www.CampMichigan.org

Printed in the United States of America

ISBN 978-0-9994332-4-9
Category —Michigan Travel

Cover Photos:
Ludington boardwalk
Harrison campground
Hartwick Pines chapel
Burt Lake bench sunset
Tawas Point Lighthouse

"I learn by going where I have to go "
Theodore Roethke

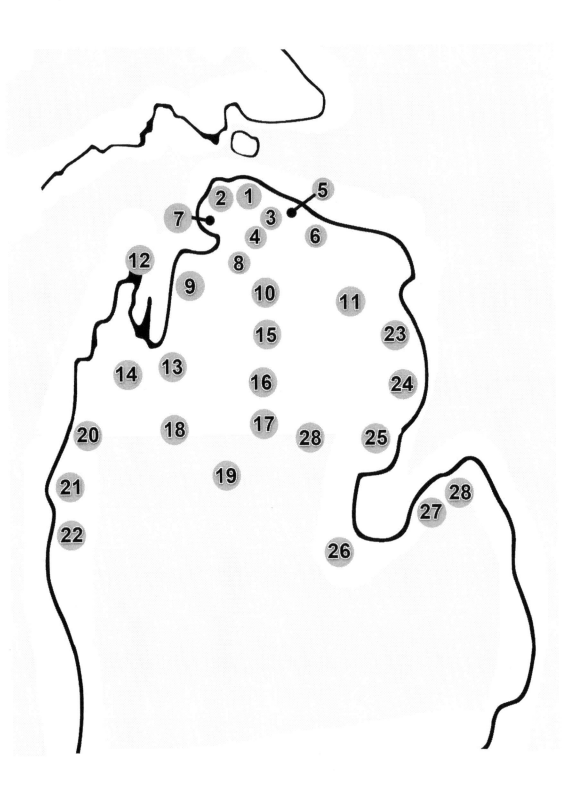

Introduction

In the late 70s and early 80s I went camping as a kid with my parents in the state parks. Back in those days we stayed in an old army surplus canvas tent. My dad had a boat so we camped in a tent so we could still tow our boat. After high school I went camping with my friends as it was a cheap place to hang out with a place to stay. After my wife and I got married in the mid 90s we got a small used pop up. After the kids were born at the turn of the century we purchased a new large pop up and used it for 17 years until my son graduated school. Now we have moved up to a small travel trailer. I have experienced camping at several parks in all kinds of weather, and I wrote this book to share my love for camping and experiences exploring in the Michigan State Parks.

Over the years, the parks have changed and I have kept track of areas in the different parks that I like. I am not going to give you specific site numbers and tell you that they are the best since different people like different things. Our pop up did not have a bathroom and when we camped in it being near a bathroom was important. Our new trailer has a bathroom and now I would prefer to be further away from the the foot traffic going to and from the facilities. Some people like to be near the beach, others like the shade. As you see, its hard to nail down the perfect site but some areas are better than others. That being said or at least written, I would rather be on any campsite relaxing than having to be at work.

Michigan's state park system was established in 1919 after the passage of Public Act 218, which created the Michigan State Park Commission to acquire lands for public use. In the early days of the parks tourists traveled down primitive roads in their Tin Lizzies to camp in a tent. During the depression, visitors and funding declined. Franklin D. Roosevelt's New Deal provided funding and jobs for workers who built stone and log buildings in the parks, most of which are still being used today. After the expressways were constructed taking travelers with motorhomes and travel trailers to the parks electricity was added but still limited. In the 90s the electrical system was upgraded at most of the parks for modern RVs to run conveniences such as air conditioning.

The state parks in Michigan provide campers with decent amenities making them extremely popular with tourists not only from Michigan but also from other states in the Midwest. The state run parks are not as fancy as some of the upscale RV resorts, but offer a relaxing camping experience. Most of the parks offer 30 amp power posts per site. The average campsite size is about 30 x 30 feet and usually a dirt surface. Some are grassy and others may have a gravel or a paved trailer pad. The bathroom buildings tend to be brick construction with tiled showers and toilet area. They may not be fancy but they are usually clean. Most of the restrooms throughout the park system are about the same level of comfort except for a few parks that have newer "green" eco-friendly bathrooms that have been built in recent years.

Many parks are on a lake and have a beach as well as a boat ramp. Others have hiking trails or even a lighthouse. There is a lot to love about each park, but of course some parks are not as popular as others.

I did my best to give an honest review of each park, both the positives and the negatives. Any opinions in this book are solely my opinions and do not reflect that of any other person, private organization or government entity. I tried to be as accurate as possible at the time this book was published.

Fees

Entrance fee
You will need a pass to enter a state park. If you are a Michigan resident an annual recreation passport can be added to your license plate tab for $11 when renewing it. If you purchase one at the park it will be $16. Non Michigan residents pay $32 for an annual pass or $9 for a day pass.

Campsite Fees
Campsite fees vary from park to park and the type of campsite. Rustic sites are usually about $9 to $12. The most common type of campsite is a modern one with 30 amp electricity which runs anywhere from $25 to $37 a night.
Some campgrounds have full hookup with electric, water, and sewer hookup and those usually cost about $45 a night.
If you make a reservation for a campsite there is an $8 reservation fee online or a $10 fee if you make one over the phone.

Basic Rules

• Check in is at 3:00pm
• Checkout is at 1:00 pm
• One trailer and one tent per site or no trailer and multiple tents to accommodate up to six people
• Two vehicles per site
• Six un-related people per site or one family
• Quiet time is 10:00 pm
• Dogs must be on a six foot leash at all time.
• Dogs may not be left unattended.

The Michigan DNR will give you a complete list of rules when you check in, or you can find them on their website. www.michigan.gov/dnr/

Typical Campsite

The average campsite at a Michigan State Park is about 30 foot by 30 feet and has a concrete fire-pit ring and a picnic table. The sites vary in size but are usually large enough for a trailer and a tow vehicle with a little room left over for a tent or a second car.
The surface is usually dirt since the parks are used a lot in the summer. Some have gravel or even paved asphalt parking pads.
The description on the DNR website will describe if the site is level or unlevel. Understand that if a site is described as level that does not mean it is perfectly level like a poured concrete pad in an RV resort. It means that is appears level to the eye. Leveling blocks may still be needed under trailer wheels. If a site is deemed unlevel, it is probably on a hill and it can be potentially difficult to level a trailer. I would recommend staying away from an unlevel site if you have a trailer, especially if it is a large trailer. Typically, unlevel sites are for tent camping and may be described that way on the DNR's reservation website.

Modern Campsite

A modern campsite and campground has a bathroom building with flush toilets and showers. The campsites have either 30 amp or 50 amp electrical posts. Some sites even have full hookup.

Semi-modern Campsite

A semi modern campsite and campground has either electricity available or a bathroom building with flush toilets. Usually it's electricity, the bathrooms are winterized in the fall and pit toilets are used during the semi modern camping season. The sanitation station will probably be closed during the semi-modern season also.

Rustic Campsite

Rustic campsites do not have electricity and only a pit toilet is available. Usually only a hand pump is available for water and a sanitation station is not available

Making Reservations

Michigan is one of the most popular states for recreational vehicles and camping which can make acquiring reservations at your favorite Michigan State Park difficult. The current online reservation system is the best and most intricate one the DNR has created. It has come a long way from the days when you had to send in a check by mail to hold a spot so you could choose your site from what was available when you got to the campground. The current system lets you choose a date to see what is available in the state or you can pick a specific campground and see what dates are open. I am not associated with the state parks and have no "inside knowledge" but I have learned some

tips and tricks over the years to help with getting your reservations. If you don't already know it, here is the website to make reservations:
www.midnrreservations.com

Make them as soon as you can

The Michigan DNR will let you make reservations for a campsite six month to the day before your arrival date. If you want to make reservations for the 4th of July you should be making them the 4th of January. The system starts taking reservations at 8 am weekdays and 9 am weekends. For the most popular parks like Ludington, you will need to try to make reservations when the system opens for the day since the park is so popular.

Be flexible

Most people want to stay at the most popular sites in the most popular parks during holiday weekends. If you are like me and are restricted by when you can take your vacation because of work, you need to be flexible on where you stay so you can find a campsite. It may not be exactly what you want, but a day relaxing next to a campfire is better than not camping at all. The system lets you pick your dates and then you can look on a map to see what campgrounds are available for those dates. Make sure the pull down with the lists of all the campgrounds is set to the Michigan State Parks and it will show all the parks on the map and whether they have availability

Maybe you are retired and the dates you go camping are not that important, but you have a specific campground you want to stay at. You can search for dates the campground has openings. If a site you want is already reserved you can click on it and see the schedule of what days it is reserved and what days it's available.

Do your research

If you are going to book six months to the day #SMTTD be sure to check the campground map ahead of time. Have a site or even a couple of sites picked out so you are not trying to pick one while other people are reserving sites. You can check the night before you make your reservations to see what is available.

Go a day early

If you go a day earlier than planned, you can possibly make your reservation before others do since the system lets you reserve sites six months before your arrival date. I know this is not always feasible, but for instance, on a holiday weekend if you take Friday off from work you can go on Thursday and may have a better chance to get a campsite than someone who is arriving on Friday.

Please be considerate. Since the system will let you make reservations starting with the day you arrive and will let you reserve up to 15 days, some people make reservations early to get the site they want. Then, later on, cancel the early days. I don't do this and although it is legal, it is really inconsiderate, like people who cut in front of you while waiting in line. The DNR has changed the cancellation policy to help curb this. I am not sure how many people do this and I don't think it as common as people think. I know there are a lot of retirees who stay at the Michigan State Parks and they are fortunate enough to be able to camp for two weeks at a time. There are also more and more Michiganders camping so some of the parks are just really difficult to acquire reservations at.

Going Mid-week

Campsites are usually full on the weekends so if you are planning a week long stay at a park for summer vacation it can be hard to get a site with a Friday arrival date. I know you don't want to give up a time for relaxing but I have waited until Sunday to head to the campground. You may have more options to choose from since the park may not be as busy during the week as it is during the weekend. Plus, traveling on Sunday the traffic is not as heavy as you will be going the opposite direction from the weekend crowd. This gives you all day Saturday to pack your trailer for the trip.

Check for cancellations

If the park you want to get into is full, keep checking back to see if a site has become available. People with reservations six months out have to wait to cancel or alter their reservations five months before arrival. Check five months before your plans, and you may be able to snag a recently canceled reservation before someone else does.

Check for Festivals and Events

Don't forget to check on local events happening near the campground you are considering. Events like the Cherry Festival in Traverse City or the Cheeseburger Festival in Caseville will cause the nearby parks to have a large number of people at them. If there is a festival happening the weekend of your stay, whether or not you plan to attend the festival, be sure to book early. Don't forget about the harvest festivals most parks have in the fall. They are very popular and fill up the campground. If you want to go to one or prefer to avoid them, check the list of events on the DNR website.

Trailer Size

Be sure to check the pull-down menu for trailer size. If you have a smaller trailer like I do, make sure you don't have a larger one selected otherwise it will only show you sites available for a larger trailer. You can also use the pull down to find larger campsites. If you set the pull down to a large trailer like 40 feet then you can find out which sites are larger but still use a smaller trailer on it.

The Best Campsites

When making reservations and it comes time to pick a campsite you want to pick the best site. It's always an agonizing decision especially if you have never visited the park. It would be nice to have a list of campsites that are "the best". The challenge with making a list is that everyone has different requirements that make one site better than the other. Some people want a site with plenty of sunshine, other like plenty of trees with lots of shade. Most people like to be near the water but not everyone wants to be near the beach. For people who camp in a tent or pop up without a toilet it's nice to be near a bathroom building. If you have a trailer with a bathroom maybe you prefer to be in a quiet section of the park away from the bathroom and the foot traffic that travels to and from it.

Instead of giving you a list of campsites that I think are the best, I describe the campground and the different areas so you can make an informed decision as to which one works best for you.

Things to consider when choosing a site

How far from the bathroom is the site? It's nice to be closer to the bathroom but it also brings more people walking past your campsite. If your site is across from the bathroom even though it is poor etiquette to cut through another persons campsite people do it and if you are near the bathroom it is more likely to happen.

How close is the beach? If you like spending a lot of time at the beach and have a lot of stuff to haul to it, you may like being near the beach or water. Being near the water and beach usually means less trees and more sunshine. It may also be noisy with kids playing in the water or people playing volleyball. After going through a storm while camping near the lake, I don't like being near it during the spring and fall. It can be cold and it's difficult to relax with a strong wind coming off the lake.

The campsites on the outer perimeter of the campground can be good campsites because you will not have anyone camped behind you, just be careful that there is not a fence, steep hill or dropoff limiting the depth of the campsite.

Sites to avoid

Near a footpath to the bathroom or beach because of all the people walking next to your campsite and inevitably people will cut through your site instead of using the footpath.

Next to the playground. If you have young kids full of energy it might be a good thing to be near the playground. If you like peace and quiet you probably don't want to be near the playground with all the kids running around hopped up on sugar and screaming their heads off. Not that there's anything wrong with it because that's what kids do at the campground.

If the campground is near a road, especially a busy road, it's nice to be as far away from the road as possible to get away from the noise of the traffic.

Firewood

All the parks sell firewood, either at the rangers station where you check in or at a park store. The Michigan DNR prefers that you purchase campfire wood from the park and don't transport it. This is to help curb the spread of diseases and insects like the emerald ash borer. The park usually sells wood by the bundle which can be expensive if you burn a lot of wood. Stores and individuals near the park usually sell firewood. If you need a lot of fire wood, you can find someplace selling a large bundle or face cord for a decent price.

In the past, the DNR had plans to require all visitors to purchase firewood in the park, and prohibit anyone from transporting it into the campground. They have decided to allow people to bring in locally purchased wood, but they may enact the policy in the future.

Camp Stores

Some campgrounds have camp stores in a separate building or in the beach house. They usually have the basic grocery necessities along with snacks. Some have ice cream and a concession stand with hot food. The stores are usually not run by the park. The space is leased to a private individual or company to operate in from year to year. The store may change because the lease has changed. If you stay at a park, expect the store may be different than it was when you last stayed at that park.

Park Icons

Water		Picnic Tables	
Electric		Picnic Shelter	
Modern Bathroom		Dog Beach	
Sanitation Station		Snowmobiling	
Playground		Cross Country Skiing	
Camp Store		Vault Toilet	
Swimming Beach		ORV Trails	
Kayaking and Canoeing		Fishing	
Full Hookup Sites		Boat Launch	
Hunting		Lighthouse	
Mini Cabin		Bicycling	
Lodge		Hiking	

Map Icons

	Modern Bathroom Building		Store
	Dump Station		Playground
	Yurt		Mini Cabin
	Water		Pit Toilet
	Lodge		Tee Pee

Cheboygan State Park

4490 Beach Rd
Cheboygan MI, 49721
231-627-2811

76 modern campsites
1 lodge
2 tee pees
3 rustic cabins
1250 Acres

Semi Modern opens beginning of April
Modern opens mid May
Modern closes mid October
Campgrounds close late November

Cheboygan State Park is located near the tip of the Lower Peninsula and with 1250 acres it has plenty of room for you to go exploring. The campground has 77 campsites and the town of Cheboygan is only a few miles away.

Pros
- Near Cheboygan
- Lots of Hiking trails
- Near the Tip of the Lower Peninsula

Cons
- Beach is a long distance from the campground
- Lots of wetlands in the park for mosquitoes
- Only 20 amp electrical service available

Campground

Cheboygan State Park is a large park, but it has a small campground, with only 77 campsites compared to other state parks in the region. One issue for those who may want to run an air conditioner in their RV is that the sites only have 20 amp electrical service. The roads in the park are gravel, the sites are marked by numbers on the firepits. The campsites vary from open sunlight to shady and secluded so make sure to read the description of the site when making reservations. The campground is flat and sites are mostly grassy. It sits along Lake Huron in Duncan Bay. Campsites are near the water but the area is somewhat marshy and the shoreline has cattails growing up in the water. It would be good for kayaking, but not really for swimming. It does offer a nice quiet place to stay for family vacations to the Straights of Mackinaw area.

Cheboygan Campground

Reservations

Other than maybe holidays you should not need to make reservations too early. There are several other campgrounds in the area and Cheboygan seems to be one of the least favored among them. With Aloha State Park

not far away most people opt to stay there first. Cheboygan is a good place to check for those last minute trips, but as always, with any state park, you should make reservations as soon as you can.

Bathrooms

The campground only has one bathroom building so don't let that be a deciding factor when picking your site. It's an older wooden structure, but maintained fairly well.

Cheboygan campground bathroom building

Cell Service

Cell service is dependent on where you are at in the park since it is such a large park but it is not a strong signal if you do get one. When I was at the beach and the campground I did not get a signal. I would plan on having limited if any service if you stay at Cheboygan State Park. Be sure to check your messages and email when you are in town.

Beach and Boating

The beach is on Duncan Bay, a small bay off Lake Huron. It's a nice sandy beach with a large beach house with an attached pavilion. It's not a large beach, but then again there are not a lot of campsites at the campground. Unfortunately it is a long distance to the beach from the campground. On the map it's not far, but there are wetlands separating the swimming area from the campsites. It's about a two mile drive by car to the designated beach area. The beach house does have flush toilets and running water.

You can launch a small boat such as a canoe or kayak in some areas of the park, but the park does not have a boat launch for large boats on trailers.

Cheboygan beach house

Beach at Cheboygan State Park

11

Shopping and Restaurants

The park does not have a store, but Cheboygan is only a few miles away with everything from a small convenience store to a Walmart and Home Depot. Cheboygan will have just about anything you may need. The downtown area has some nice little stores along with some great restaurants if you want to take a break from cooking.

Things To Do

The park has six miles of hiking trails, many of them along the Lake Huron shoreline. One of the trails lead to an old lighthouse foundation. The seclusion of Duncan Bay is ideal for kayakers and canoers to enjoy some time on the water. The park is only about 15 miles away from Mackinaw City along with all the tourist attractions it has to offer for a summer vacation. There are a few lighthouses in the area including the Range Light in Cheboygan and the Crib Light that marks the entrance to the Cheboygan River.

Playground at the beach

The old lighthouse

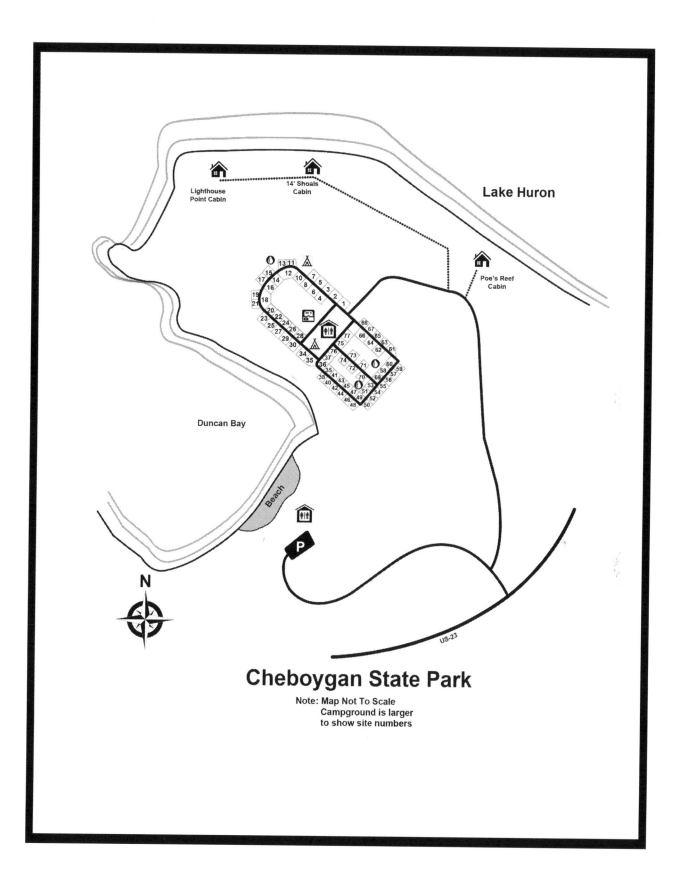

Lighthouse
Point Cabin

14' Shoals
Cabin

Lake Huron

Poe's Reef
Cabin

Duncan Bay

Beach

P

N

US-23

Cheboygan State Park

Note: Map Not To Scale
Campground is larger
to show site numbers

Wilderness State Park

903 Wilderness Park Drive
Carp Lake MI, 49718
231-436-5381

250 modern campsites
18 full hookup campsites
9 rustic cabins
10512 Acres

Semi Modern opens end of March

Modern opens mid May

Modern closes mid October

Campgrounds close beginning of December

Wilderness State Park is a piece of heaven on the west side of the tip of the Lower Peninsula. With over 10,500 acres of land and 26 miles of Lake Michigan shoreline any outdoor adventurer will love this park. The park offers a variety of camping opportunities, including 250 modern campsites that are divided into three units, as well as 18 full hook-up sites and 25 walk in tent sites. Six rustic cabins and three rustic bunkhouses are also available for you to stay in and enjoy what the park has to offer.

Pros
- Near Mackinaw city
- Some full hookup sites
- Large park to explore

Cons
- Busy park in the summer
- Long drive to store
- Older bathrooms

Campground

The campground area of the park is divided up into four different sections.

The New Campground

The DNR has recently added this section and for some reason, they have yet to give it an official name. The sites are letters instead of numbers and have full hookup sites with gravel pads for parking your trailer. There are not many trees in the middle of the campground so it has plenty of sunshine. Walk in tent sites are on both sides of the full hook-up sites. The ranger station and a new bathroom building are also located in this section of the campground.

The Pines Campground

The Pines Campground is heavily wooded with plenty of trees for shade. The bathroom building is older, but has had some recent work done to it. The Pines area is fully paved with paved camping pads to park your RV or trailer on. If you have a large trailer and can't get a full hookup I would suggest the Pines Campground.

The East Lakeshore Campground

The East Lakeshore Canmpground has dirt roads with well worn campsites. This is the older section of the park but still really popular since it is next to Lake Michigan. The sites here are smaller than the ones in the Pines section. Good for smaller trailers or tents.

The West Lakeshore Campground

The West Lakeshore Campground at the time of publishing this book was undergoing extensive renovations and was closed to the public. It looked like they were building all new roads and updating the electrical system. Instead of speculating what it will be like, check out the DNR website for more info. I hope to have updates in future editions of this book.

Pines Campground

Reservations

The parks proximity to Mackinaw City makes it extremely popular with families on vacation. You will want to make reservations as soon as you can. Most site are reserved six months to the day, especially the full hookup sites and the sites near Lake Michigan.

Bathrooms

The new section of the park with full hookups has a newer bathroom, but the other bathrooms in the campground are getting a little dated. I think the bathroom at the Pines is better than the one at the East Lakeshore campground. With the construction going on at the West Lakeshore campground I am unsure of what that bathroom will be like once the renovations are finished.

Bathroom Building in the Pines Campground

Cell Service

I have AT&T as my provider and I don't have any kind of a signal at Wilderness State Park. I know people who have Verizon and they are able to get a little bit of a signal. I would plan on little to no service no matter who your provider is.

Beach and Boating

The main beach at Wilderness is more of a "natural" beach with grasses and plants growing up through the sand. It's not like the large Lake Michigan beaches in the southern parts of the state with lots of sand. There are areas to lay out and enjoy getting sun burnt, at least that's what I get instead of a tan.

A dog beach is located south of the designated swimming beach for mans best friend to cool off on a hot summer day.

The park does have a boat launch on Lake Michigan. I have never seen anyone anchor a boat near the shoreline, but that may be because of the waves on Lake Michigan. If you have a boat, I would plan on taking it out of the water when you are not using it.

Shopping and Restaurants

Near the entrance of the state park is the Cecil Trading Post that has most of your basic needs. Although it is near the entrance, it is still a few miles to get to the store from the campground. If you want to go to Mackinaw City it's about 15 miles from the campground. Its deceiving how far away Mackinaw City is because the park is so large and the campground is in the middle of it. Strangely, as big of a town as Mackinaw City is, it only has a small grocery store. There are plenty of bars and restaurants to choose from if you want to take a break from the grill. If you want to go to a Walmart or another big box store you need to go to Cheboygan, which is about 30 miles from the park.

Things To Do

What makes Wilderness S.P. so popular is the variety of things to do in the surrounding area. Besides hiking its miles of trails and exploring the Lake Michigan shoreline, there are many nearby places to visit. The most obvious are Mackinaw City and Mackinac Island. You can visit McGulpin Point Lighthouse and climb the tower to get a one of a kind view of the Mighty Mac, or you can do some stargazing at the nearby Headlands International Dark Sky Park. If you want to go for an adventure Cross Village is not far away if you take the back roads to it. You could easily stay at Wilderness for a week and still not see everything the area has to offer. I guess you will just have to go back or stay at one of the other nearby state parks.

Beach on Lake Michigan

17

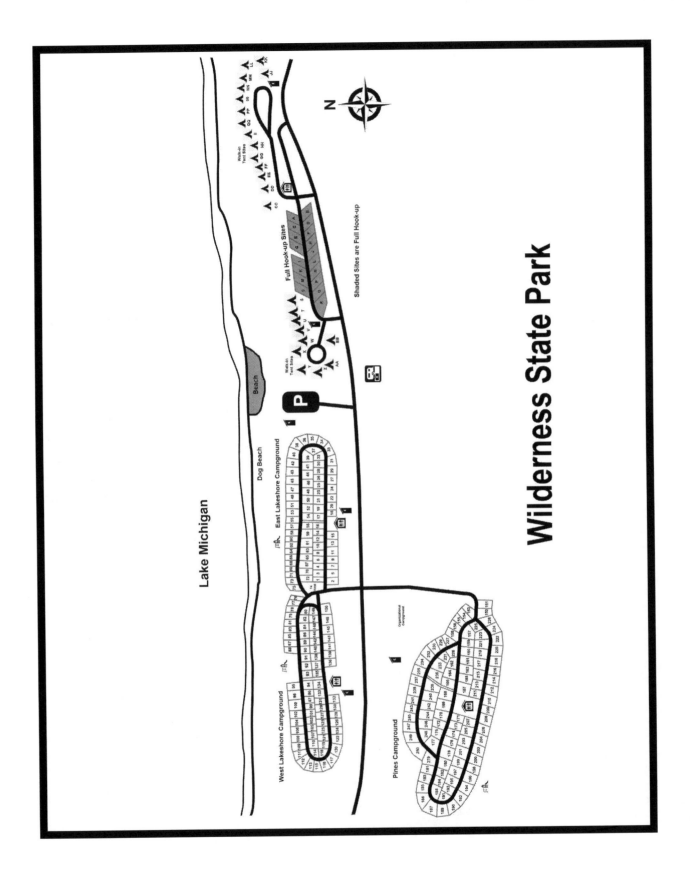

Wilderness State Park

Aloha State Park

4347 Third Street
Cheboygan MI, 49721
231-625-2522

283 campsites
172 acres

Modern Camping Opens beginning of
April and closes the end of October

Aloha does not have semi modern
facilities

Aloha State Park is about six miles south of
Cheboygan on Mullet Lake. With a lagoon in
the middle of the campground and situated on
the Inland Waterway, it's a favorite among
boaters and fisherman. It's location in
Northern Michigan makes it an ideal spot for a
family vacation.

Pros
- Boat lagoon
- Grassy sites
- Located near Mackinaw City

Cons
- Little shade
- Long distance from southern Michigan

Aloha's grassy campsites

Campground

The campground has nice grassy sites but few trees. In the hot summer months if you may want to bring an extra dining canopy or E Z up for more shade, especially if you do not have an RV with an awning.

The most popular sites are the ones along the lake towards the north end of the park. Not only do people like the lake view but these sites are the only sites with large trees and some shade. The sites around the lagoon are popular with boaters because they can pull their boat up right to their campsites. The sites near the lake, in the middle section are popular because they are closer to the beach. If you stay at Aloha, one thing to be prepared for is the sites flooding or getting muddy in a heavy downpour. It's rare but, I have been to the park during a thunderstorm and drainage is not good in the campground.

Waterfront Campsites

Reservations

Aloha is a popular park, but there are a lot of other state parks in the area and sites can be available for reservations in late winter and early spring. You should plan on six months to the day for holidays. If you want a campsite near the lake or lagoon you will want to book those six months to the day. If you are looking for a campground in the Northern Lower Peninsula for a last minute trip, it's worth checking Aloha for availability.

Bathrooms

All three bathroom buildings in the park are identical. They are older bathrooms but well maintained. They are your typical state park bathrooms. Nothing fancy but they are acceptable for most visitors. Since all the bathrooms are the same, it shouldn't be a factor in deciding which site to pick while making reservations in the campground.

One of three identical bathrooms in the campground

Cell Service

The campground is near the town of Cheboygan so I had a few bars of service. The signal was not strong, but it worked well enough for making phone calls and texts.

Beach and Boating

The beach is nice and sandy although it seems a little small for the size of the park. You can access the lake along the shoreline if you have a campsite next to the lake so you probably won't use the designated beach. The day use beach and picnic area are next to the entrance of the park.

This park is probably the best park in the state park system for boaters. It has a nice boat launch and plenty of trailer parking. The park also has a large lagoon where you can tie your boat up while at your campsite.

Campground beach

Boat Lagoon

Shopping and Restaurants

The park does not have a store, but there is a large party store right outside the entrance of the campground. If you want to go to a big box store Cheboygan is about 6 miles away. Besides shopping Cheboygan has a plethora of restaurants to eat at so if you don't feel like cooking you should find something that will suit your taste. Downtown Cheboygan has some nice shops to explore. You are about 20 miles from Mackinaw City.

Things To Do

Besides hanging out on the beach or fishing in your boat, you can go hiking in the nearby Black Mountains or Cheboygan State Park and look for the ruins of the old lighthouse. If you want to do the tourist thing you can head over to the island (Mackinac Island of course). Mullet Lake is part of the Inland Waterway which goes from Cheboygan to Alanson near Petoskey. The campground is a nice place to camp if you are going to travel the waterway over the course of two days.

Convenience store outside of entrance to the park

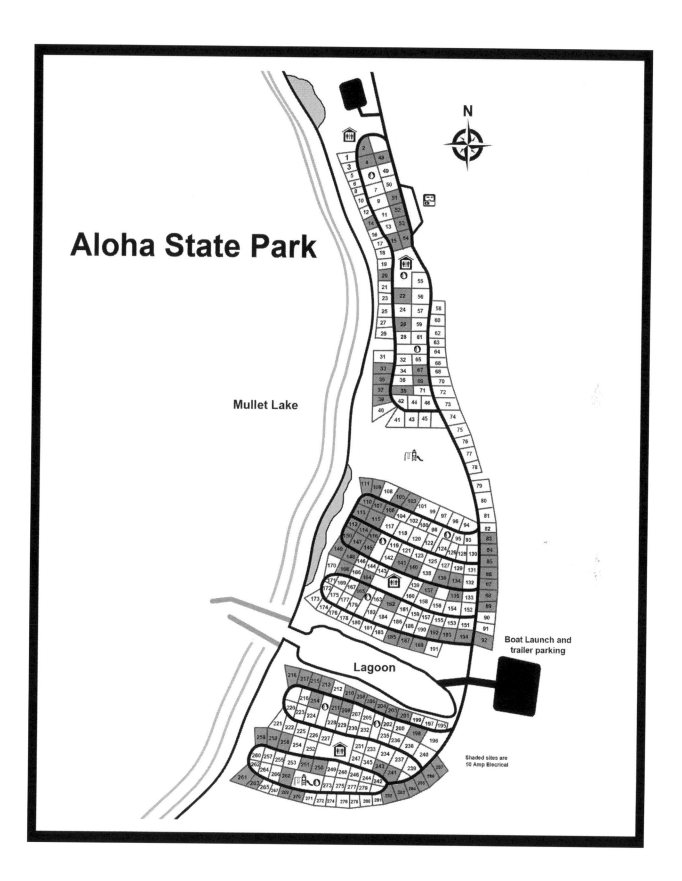

Aloha State Park

Mullet Lake

Lagoon

Boat Launch and
trailer parking

Shaded sites are
50 Amp Elecrical

23

Burt Lake State Park

6635 State Park Dr.
Indian River MI, 49749
231-238-9392

306 campsites
406 acres

Semi modern opens beginning of April

Modern opens mid May

Modern closes mid October

Campground closes for season end of November

You've heard the saying "location, location, location" and I think the best thing about Burt Lake State Park is its location in the Lower Peninsula. The park is centrally located in Northern Michigan which makes it easy to make day trips to many popular tourist destinations, such as Petoskey or Mackinaw City. Located near I-75 the park is easy to get to especially if you have a large trailer. It's a wonderful park if you are looking for someplace to camp for a week or two.

Pros
- Centrally located in the northern lower peninsula
- Near I-75
- Grocery store nearby
- Large sandy beach

Cons
- Worn campsites with dirt ground
- Older bathrooms
- Long drive from southern Michigan

Campground

The park is one of the larger parks in the state park system in terms of total number of campsites, with 306 of them. A few years ago the park removed some sites reducing the total number while enlarging the sites to accommodate larger RVs. The sites nearest the lake have few trees so they will not have any shade. A few rows away from the lake, the sites are wooded and most will have full shade. Most sites are level but well used and are mostly a dirt surface. I would stay away from sites 243 thru 256 as there is a hill in the middle of them and I would not want to set up a trailer on them. The sites in the back of the park around 224 can be noisy on Sunday mornings since the Cross In The Woods shrine is next to the park and you can hear the morning worship.

Reservations

Burt Lake is not as popular as Ludington or a handful of other parks, but it is still rather popular. For holiday weekends you definitely want to make reservations six months to the day. For other dates between Memorial and Labor Day you can probably reserve sites three months before but to be safe I would make reservations as soon as you can. The sites closest to the the lake and beach are the most popular and fill up fast all summer long

Cell Service

AT&T and Verizon work well in the park but I know some people who have Sprint and for some reason there is no signal available.

Campsite near beach

North bathroom building

East bathroom building

West bathroom Building

Bathrooms

The bathrooms at Burt Lake vary from recently built to some that are rather old. The two bathroom buildings farthest from the lake are newer buildings but not brand new I would say they are about 20 years old and are the typical state park bathroom. They have a covered walkway with the bathrooms on one side and the other side of the walkway and five shower stalls on the other. The bathrooms closer to the lake are older bathrooms which I am guessing were built in the 50s. They are not as nice as the newer bathrooms. When I have camped at Burt Lake the staff does an OK job of cleaning the bathrooms, although I think it depends on how busy the park is.

Middle bathroom building

Beach and Boating

The beach at Burt Lake is one of the best beaches in the northern Lower Peninsula. It's large with hundreds of feet of shoreline. The water is clean, clear and has a shallow sandy bottom. It's great for little kids or for setting your chair in the water and relaxing. The beach is kept raked and cleaned. There can be a large crowd of people from the large day use parking lot, but the size of the beach can handle a large crowd.

A separate swimming area fenced off for dogs is south of the beach so they can have a chance to cool off on a hot day.

The park has a boat launch, but not a lagoon like Aloha State Park. Most people anchor their boat off shore in the shallow waters south of the beach. The park is near the mouth of the Indian River, which is part of the Inland Waterway that goes from Alanson to Cheboygan.

Pet area and beach

Beach on Burt Lake

Shopping and Restaurants

Right outside the park exit is the town of Indian River. Ken's grocery store is less than a quarter mile from the entrance and if you're in a motorhome without a tow car, you could walk or bike to it in a few minutes. If you don't feel like cooking there are some good restaurants in the area along with fast food including McDonald's, Burger King, and Subway. If you like to finish a hot summer day with ice cream Indian River has you covered. There are a few different places to get your favorite flavor. My favorite is Drosts and their blueberry waffle cone. If you want to go to a big box store like Walmart or Meijer it's about a 30 min drive to either Cheboygan or Petoskey. There is also a park store in the beach house with snacks, ice cream, bags of ice and a small selection of groceries. The prices are a little more than in town, but it is convenient. If shopping is your thing, there are a few nice gift shops in Indian River and you are not far away from some of the best shopping in downtown Petoskey and Mackinaw City.

Things to do

The park has a one mile foot trail in the park for hiking, but I would say Burt Lake S.P. is not the best choice if hiking is what you love to do. The Sturgeon River flows through the northern edge of the park and is ideal for kayaking, tubing and canoeing. If you don't have your own equipment there are a few places in Indian River you can rent from that will take you upstream to drop you off. Indian River Golf Club is just north of town if you're looking for somewhere to hit some balls around. To the south of the park, on Old 27 is the ORV Trailhead if you are looking for somewhere to ride your ATV or dirt bike.

Park store and beach house

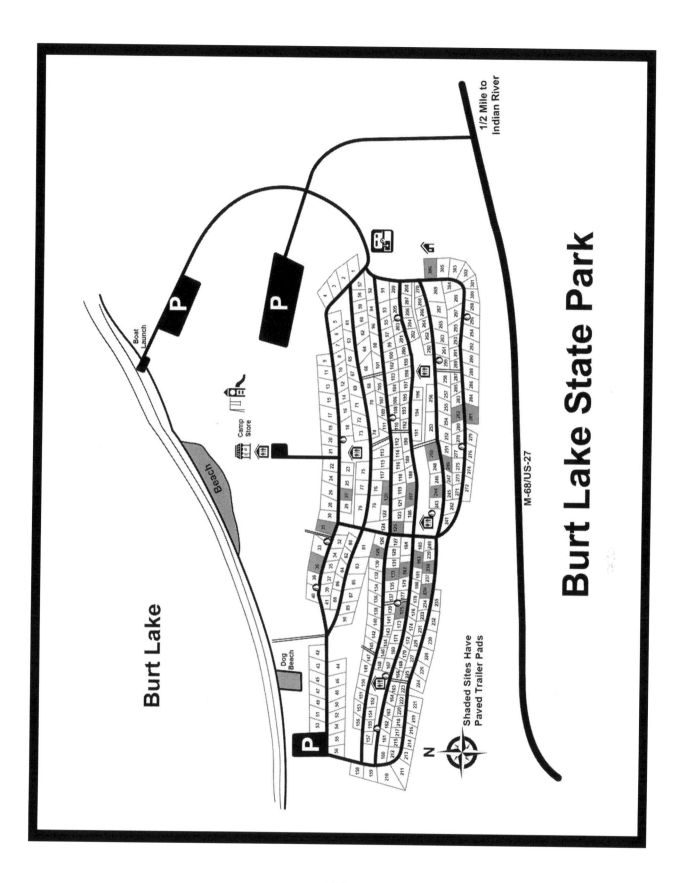

Burt Lake

Burt Lake State Park

29

Onaway State Park

3622 N. M-211
Onaway MI, 49765
989-733-8279

82 modern campsites
1 cabin
158 acres

Semi Modern opens beginning of April

Modern opens the middle of April

Modern closes the middle of October

Semi modern closes late November.

Onaway State Park is situated along the shores of Black Lake north of Onaway Michigan. It is a heavily wooded park and if you like to fish and want a quiet park to stay at I think you will enjoy Onaway State Park.

Pros
- Wooded Sites with Shade
- Boat Launch
- Newer Shower Building
- Waterfront Campsites

Cons
- Small Beach
- Shared Power Posts
- Small park
- Small Sites that can be difficult to fit large trailers

Campground

The campground at Onaway is an older campground with gravel roads throughout the park. The sites are nice and shaded but also have a lot of trees on them so it can be challenging to get a larger trailer to fit. The campground is also hilly and unlevel so be sure to bring some leveling boards if you have a trailer or motorhome. Multiple campsites share electrical posts and if you are between posts you will need a long power cord to reach the post. I would recommend at least 100 feet of cord. Sites 1 through 24 are on a loop near the lake, with sites 1 through 15 directly on the shoreline. The shoreline along the sites is rocky so you won't be able to pull a boat up to your campsite, but you could probably launch a kayak or rowboat. One drawback of being near the lake is the park only has a vault toilet for the sites in that area. Most of the sites are rather small and you will have to "parallel" park your trailer to get it on the lot. When making reservations be sure to check your trailer size as there are about 35 sites that can accommodate large trailers.

Reservations

Onaway State Park is not as popular as some of the other nearby parks making it somewhat easy to get a reservation. As always, for holiday weekends you should book your site as early as you can, preferably six months to the day. For the rest of the weekends you can usually get a site a few weeks in advance if not the day before. This is a great campground for a last minute trip. The big issue is trailer size. If you want to stay here and you have a large trailer, sites are limited and you want to reserve the large sites as soon as you can.

Lakefront campsite at Onaway

Wooded campsites at Onaway

Bathrooms

The bathroom building is an older building but it is in good shape and maintained. There is only one modern building in the campground. When it is closed for cleaning, vault toilets are available across the street from the bathroom building so be sure to look at the posted cleaning times. A new building next to the bathrooms houses the showers for the campground.

Cell Service

Onaway State Park is secluded from civilization and I had a weak cell signal. If you visit, I would plan on not having cell service. If you do get a signal, that is an added bonus. If not just relax and enjoy the peace and quiet of nature.

Bathroom building

Shower building

Campground beach on Black Lake

Day use beach on Black Lake

Shopping and Restaurants

The park does not have a store but, there is a large party store right outside the entrance to the park. They have a good selection of booze and some sandwiches along with basic necessities. If you need something that the party store does not have the town of Onaway is about 7 miles away. In Onaway you will find a Subway, Dairy Queen, pizza place and some local restaurants. They also have a grocery store. If you really need something at a big box store Cheboygan is about 34 miles away.

Beach and Boating

The beach at the campground is rather small but it is a nice little sandy beach. If the beach is crowded and you want to lay out in the sun there is a nice grassy area next to the beach. The beach at the day use area looks as if it is not used much since it is covered in rocks, driftwood and woodchips. Onaway S.P. does have a nice boat ramp and being on Black Lake, I would think the park is popular with fishermen or fisherwomen.

Things To Do

Other than enjoying Black Lake, Ocqueoc Falls is only 13 miles way. If you like to hike or hunt there is a lot of state land around Black Lake including Black Mountain Recreation Area, which has miles of hiking trails.

Convenience store across from entrance

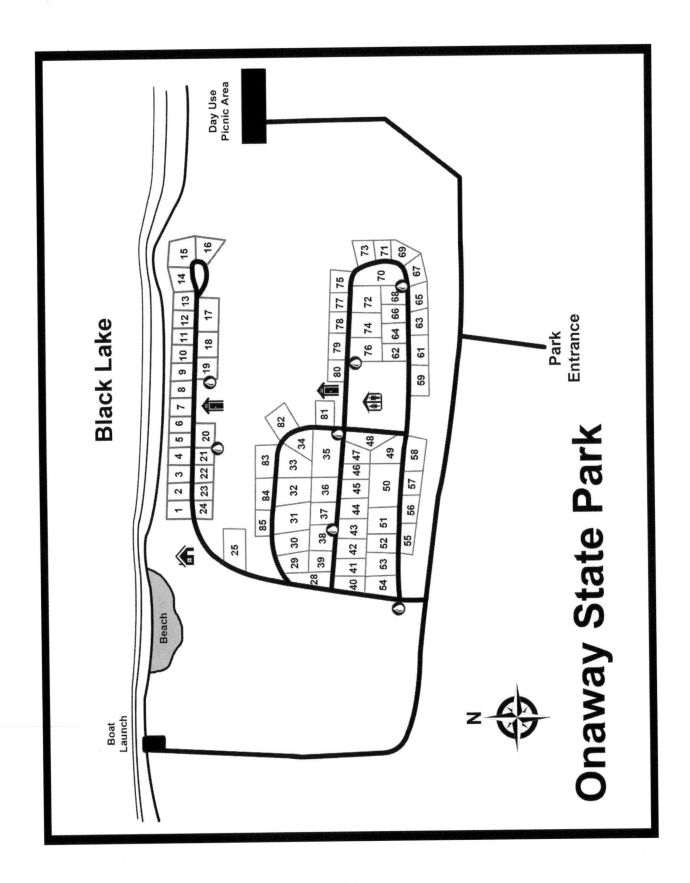

Onaway State Park

Black Lake

Boat Launch

Beach

Day Use Picnic Area

Park Entrance

N

34

Hoeft State Park

5001 US-23 North
Rogers City MI, 49779
989-734-2543

144 campsites
301 acres

Semi modern open all year

Modern opens mid May

Modern closes mid October

I am not sure why P.H. Hoeft State Park is not more popular than it is. It's a beautiful park north of Rogers City with a long sandy shoreline. It's a nature lovers paradise with wooded lots, hiking trails and it is not far from many other natural areas such as Ocqueoc Falls and Black Mountain Natural Area.

Pros
- Sandy Beach
- Near Rogers City
- Hiking Trails in the park
- Wooded and shady sites

Cons
- Some sites are hilly and unlevel
- A long drive from southern Michigan
- Limited tourist shopping and restaurants compared to west side of state
- No Boat Launch

Campground

If you are looking for a quiet peaceful place to camp, Hoeft would be a good choice. Since there are several other state parks in the area Hoeft seems to be not as popular as some of the other locations. The campground is heavily wooded and shady, but also hilly and unlevel. It can be a challenge to get a large trailer to fit on many of the campsites. Be sure to check the dimensions of the campsite when making your reservations. You will want to be sure to have leveling boards or the plastic lego thingies to pull your wheels onto to level your trailer from side to side. You will also want to make sure to have plenty of 30 amp power cord. Make sure to have a few extensions because you may need at least 100 feet to reach a power post. The campsites do not have their own individual post and are shared among multiple sites. The roads in the campground are gravel and they still use the old school posts to mark the campsites. The campsites near Lake Huron seem to be the most popular, even though they are not right on the lake and you can't see the lake from the campsites. I think people like them because it's a short walk to the beach.

Reservations

As I have said, Hoeft State Park is not as popular as other parks and is probably the least popular park in the Northern Lower Peninsula. Other than holiday weekends, I think it's rare that the park will be full. It's a great choice for those last minute trips up north. However, I would recommend getting reservations early if you have a trailer 30 feet or longer. I think there are only about 25 campsites that will accommodate a large trailer so you want to be sure to reserve one so your trailer will fit.

Wooded campground

36

Bathrooms

The bathrooms in the park are older but seem to be in rather good shape, I think it's partly because they don't get a lot of use. There are two showers in the men's bathroom and two in the women's. There can be a line for showers when the park is busy. The bathrooms are slightly different but similar in both age and construction. There is a bathroom in the north half and one in the south half of the park. If you are camped between them it gives you an option if they are cleaning one of them.

Bathroom building in north section

Bathroom building in south section

Day use beach on Lake Huron

Beach and Boating

There are two beach access locations in the park. The beach runs the entire length of the park and also has sand dunes similar to the Lake Michigan parks. The southern access to the beach is in the day use parking area. The northern access is in the campground at the northern end of the park between campsites 21 and 23. There is no dog beach in the park so if you want to take your four legged friend swimming you could probably go outside the park along the M-23 Lake Huron Shoreline. The park does not have a boat launch or a good location to beach a boat. If you have a boat, you can launch at Rogers City Marina.

Day use beach house

Cell Service

I have AT&T and my service was not very good. I had one bar some of the time. It was ok for the occasional text or phone call but I did not get enough of a signal to use the Internet. My friends that were there with Verizon did a little better but also had a weak signal. Not far away in Rogers City, I had a strong signal and if I needed to use my phone, I would do it in town before I got back to the park.

Campground Beach

Shopping and Restaurants

The campground host manages a make-shift store in the park next to the host site. It a tent like structure that is open on the weekends. If you need anything else Rogers City is about 5 miles away and just a short trip down M-23. I would say Rogers City is more of an industrial town with the quarry being nearby. It has a good marina and park, but I would not say it's an upscale tourist town like Petoskey or Traverse City. It does have some gift shops for you to do some browsing and also a grocery store and hardware store. If you need anything it's a short trip to get it.

If you want something quick to eat Rogers City does have a McDonald's and a Subway along with some local mom and pop restaurants. I ate at the campground, and I did not try any to be able to give you a recommendation.

Sears mail order kit lodge

Things To Do

The park has a couple miles of hiking trails that meander throughout its wooded area on both sides of M-23. A bike path runs from the nearby 40 Mile Point Lighthouse to Rogers City. The park has tandem bicycles available for rent. There is a nice playground for the kids to play on with recently updated playground equipment. Not far from the park is Ocqueoc Falls and the Bicentennial Pathway. If you walk along the shoreline, about a mile north of the park, you can see the Sacred Stone that was used as a navigational aid by the Native Americans.

Campground playground

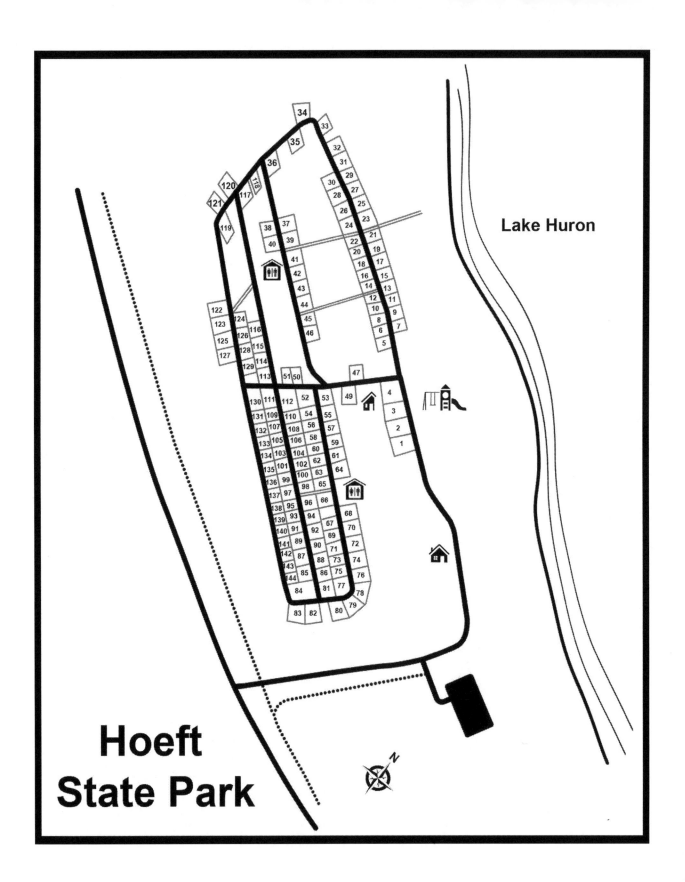

Lake Huron

Hoeft
State Park

Petoskey State Park

2475 M-119 Hwy.
Petoskey MI, 49770
231-347-2311
180 campsites
2 Mini cabins
303 acres

Modern opens beginning of May

and closes mid October

(Semi modern camping not available)

Petoskey State Park is located on Little Traverse Bay between two of the most popular tourist cities in Michigan. Besides the obvious town of Petoskey which the park is named after not far away is the picturesque town of Harbor Springs. The park is an excellent place to stay for a weekend or a week with plenty of things to do to keep any tourist happy.

Pros
- Beautiful Beach
- Between Petoskey and Harbor Springs
- Lots of places to eat and shop in the area
- Hiking trails in park

Cons
- Lots of tourists and traffic
- No boat launch
- Busy park most of the camping season

Campground

The park is divided into two different campgrounds.

Tannery Creek Campground

Tannery Creek is a larger campground and is suitable for large trailers. It's a large campground, but the bathroom building is on the side opposite the lake, so if you are camping near the lake, it will be a long walk to the bathroom. The sites have a paved pad for your trailer, and most of the sites are heavily wooded with the exception of the loop furthest away from the entrance. Most of the sites have trees between them, making them somewhat secluded. The sites closest to the lake are not next to the lake, and the area is wooded so you will not have a lake view. There is a path to access the lake so you do not have to go up to the main beach to swim and relax.

The Dunes Campground

The Dunes is closer to the entrance and has smaller sites that can be sandy. It is better suited for tents and pop ups. There may be a few sites that could accommodate a larger trailer but I would not try it. It is a nice wooded campground with the bathroom building in the middle. Paths along the campground will take you to the lake, and at the north end of the Dunes Campground is a path that leads to the main beach and beach house.

One drawback to camping at Petoskey is that the area is popular with tourists, and the road the park is located on has a steady stream of cars traveling down it all day long. It can be really difficult to pull out of the entrance. The stoplights also get backed up. Even though your destination may not be far from the park it may take some time to get to it due to traffic.

Paved campsite in Tannery Creek Campground

The Dunes bathroom building

Reservations

Petoskey State Park is an extremely popular park for camping and if you want to get a spot, you need to make reservations six months to the day. It's also popular with leaf peepers in the fall. If you want to stay here, I would recommend getting reservations as early as possible, since it is busy throughout the camping season.

Cell Service

Cell service is good. Because the campground is in a highly populated area, there are towers nearby for your phone to connect to.

Bathrooms

Each campground only has one bathroom and if you have a large trailer you will most likely be at the Tannery Creek campground. The bathroom is decent and has been maintained well. The Dunes bathroom has been renovated recently. It's not fancy, but it is a nice bathroom.

Tannery Creek bathroom building

43

Beach and Boating

Petoskey has a large sandy beach on Little Traverse Bay and it is a favorite among locals and tourists. On hot summer days there are a lot of swimmers and sun bathers, but the beach is able to accommodate them. There are some rocks in the beach and along the shoreline. You can hunt for one of the coveted Petoskey stones. If you are fortunate enough to find one consider yourself lucky, they have been picked through over the years.

The main beach has a large beach house with changing rooms and a small store with some kayak rentals available.

The park does not have a boat launch. You will have to go to either Petoskey or Harbor Springs to put your boat in the water. The park does not have a good place to tie up a boat either. You could possibly tie it up on the shoreline, but with the waves on Little Traverse Bay, you probably would not want to leave it unattended.

Shopping and Restaurants

A couple miles away on, M-31, is a grocery store, drug stores and most of the big fast food chains. On the south end of Petoskey is Meijers, Walmart and many other big box stores. It's not far away but traffic will probably be heavy. Downtown Petoskey is also a wonderful place to visit with plenty of shopping and restaurants. West of the park is the town of Harbor Springs with quint little gift shops and art galleries. A block off the main road near the library is Tom's Mom's Cookies. One of my favorite places to stop for a treat. Both towns are a great place to spend an afternoon on a rainy day.

Things To Do

The park has a few miles of hiking trails to explore. If you want to explore outside of the park take a left at the exit onto M-119 towards Harbor springs. A few miles north of Harbor Springs the Tunnel Of Trees begins. This is one of Michigan's most scenic drives passing through the village of Good Hart and ending in Cross Village. The Oden Fish hatchery, where you can tour the state owned facility to see how trout are raised, is in nearby Alanson.

Beach on Little Traverse Bay

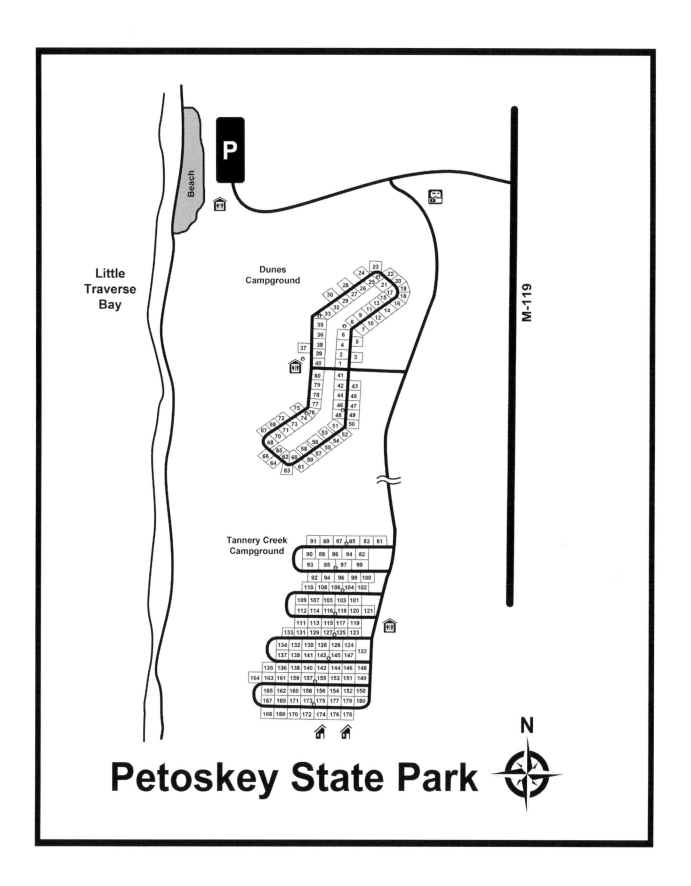

Petoskey State Park

Young State Park

2280 Boyne City Road
Boyne City MI, 49712
231-582-7523

240 campsites
2 mini cabins
563 acres

No Semi modern Camping

Modern opens the end of April

Modern closes Mid October

Young State Park located near Boyne City on Lake Charlevoix has almost anything you could want in a place to stay in Northern Michigan. It has a beautiful beach. Lots of campsites and is located near some of Michigan's best tourist towns.

Pros
- Nice beach
- Near shopping
- Boat launch

Cons
- Some bathrooms are old
- Long drive from southern Michigan

Campgrounds

The campgrounds 240 campsites are divided up into three areas. Each site has a 30 amp electrical post and some have 50 amp service.

Oak Campground

The Oak Campground has 41 campsites and the newest bathroom building. The sites are mostly wooded although some are in direct sunlight. The sites are somewhat level, but be prepared with leveling boards for under the wheels on your trailer. The sites vary in size so pay attention to the dimensions on the DNR website. Site 27 is right on the lake and sites 28, 29 and 30 are on the other side of the road from the lake. There aren't any sites across from them so you get lake access.

Terrace Campground

The Terrace Campground is next to the Oak Campground. The 43 sites are wooded and not as level. Be sure to have leveling boards. The bathroom is an older building. The boat launch is located in Terrace also. On the map some of the sites appear to be next to the water, but there are trees between the sites and the water.

Spruce Campground

The Spruce Campground is the largest section of the park with 130 campsites. It's broken up into four loops. The sites are level and rather large. The sites closer to the lake are more wooded and shady. The wooded sites are dirt with almost no grass. Farther from the lake they are more open and sunny with more grass, but they tend to get muddy if it rains heavily. The sites at the ends of the loops are larger sites because of the turns for the loop. A boardwalk in the second loop leads to the beach. If you want to be close to the beach, I recommend the Spruce Campground for large trailers.

Reservations

Young S.P. is one of the more popular parks in the northern Lower Peninsula. You should make reservations six months to the day to be sure to get a site on the weekends. You probably could get last minute reservations for the middle of the week, but I would make reservations as soon as you can.

Oak and Terrace Campgrounds on Lake Charlevoix

Oak Campground bathroom building

Cell Service

I have AT&T and the cell service was good with three bars. The internet worked well too. Being located near three major cities, I would expect to get a decent signal at the park.

Bathrooms

The bathroom at the Oak Campground is the best bathroom in the park. The Terrace Campground has an older bathroom, but it does have a row of showers. The Spruce has two identical older bathroom buildings. The outside is painted nice but the inside could use some updating. The showers are old and moldy and disappointing considering the amount of campers that use the park.

Terrace Campground bathroom building

Spruce Campground bathroom building

Beach at Spruce Campground

Beach and Boating

The park has a nice long sandy beach that stretches from the Spruce Campground to the park store near the Oak Campground. The main access to the beach is in front of the park store by the day use parking lot. There is also a boardwalk that goes to the beach from the second loop of the Spruce Campground. It's a beautiful sandy beach with nice clear water. If you love hanging out on the beach, you will love Young State Park.

A boat launch is available in the Terrace Campground. There is only enough parking for four trucks with trailers near the ramp. You will probably have to park at your site or in the main parking lot after launching your boat. The park does not have docks or a lagoon. I have seen boats anchored close to shore in the lake so I assume it's a nice sandy bottom.

Shopping and Restaurants

Young S.P. has one of the nicest camp stores I have been in. They have just about anything you want from souvenirs, t-shirts, food items to my favorite thing, ice cream. Boyne City is only a few miles away with a nice grocery store, and downtown area has a variety of gift shops and restaurants. If you need to go to a big box store Meijer, Walmart and Home Depot are about 20 minutes away in Petoskey.

Things To Do

The park has a few miles of hiking trails. The trails do not allow mountain bikes but there is a paved bicycle trail to Boyne City for cyclists to ride on. The park also has a small pond with a fishing dock. The park is not far from Charlevoix and Petoskey. Be sure to visit the general store in Horton Bay. Between Boyne City and Charlevoix is the Ironton Ferry. It's an historic car ferry that takes cars over the south arm of Lake Charlevoix. For a couple of bucks to ride across it's a fun trip. Be sure to do it after you set up your trailer. I would not want to do it with a large travel trailer.

Camp store and beach house

Mirror Lake

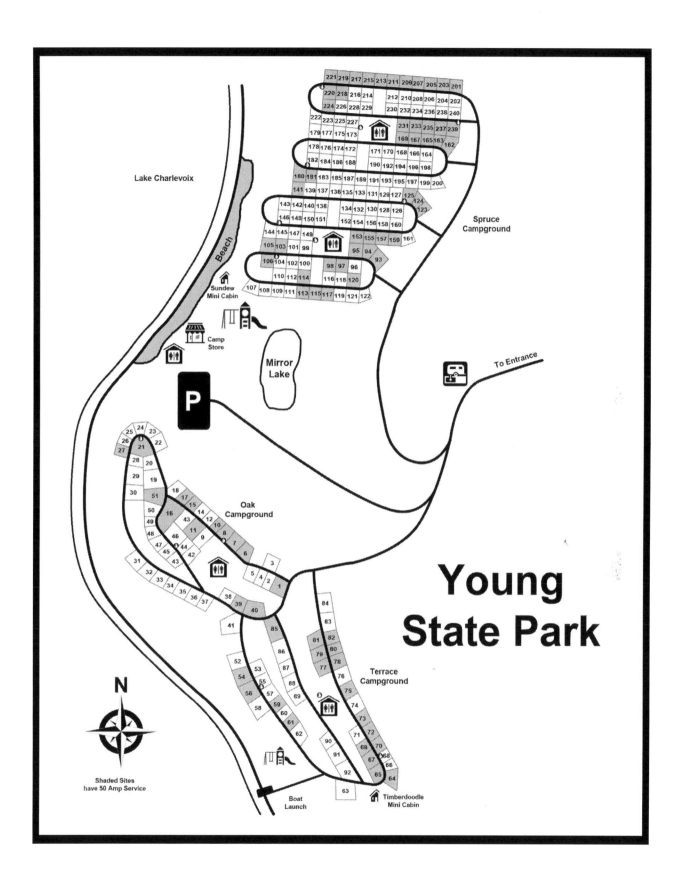

Fisherman's Island State Park

16480 Bell's Bay Road
Charlevoix MI, 49720
231-547-6641

81 rustic campsites
2678 acres

Rustic campground opens Mid April

Campground closes Mid November

No modern camping

You won't need to take a ferry to get to Fisherman's Island State Park. It's a few miles south of Charlevoix with six miles of Lake Michigan shoreline. When you arrive near the entrance to the park you wonder what it will be like since there is an enormous cement factory nearby. Once you make the turn towards the park you are greeted by tall trees and a beautiful view of Lake Michigan.

Pros
- Waterfront sites
- Large quiet park
- 6 miles of Lake Michigan shoreline

Cons
- No electricity
- Vault toilets
- No showers
- No dump station

Campground

The campground is divided into a north and south campground. All of the campgrounds are rustic and have only vault toilets. The north campground is near the entrance and the ranger station. The south campground is about a mile back from the entrance. Both are heavily wooded. The sites are spread out from each other and some can be hilly and a tight squeeze for a large trailer. Be sure to look at the description, and site dimensions when making reservations. The most popular sites are the U-shaped pull through sites on the main road. These are located right on the Lake Michigan shoreline.

Reservations

Rustic parks are usually easier to get reservations at but if you want one of the coveted lake front sites you need to reserve them as quickly as you can. Preferably six months to the day.

Bathrooms

The bathrooms are all vault toilets. I am not sure why they call them that since their contents are not valuable. They also have a men's and a women's toilet. I am not sure why there is one for each gender but there is. I have not used the women's but I can only assume it smells better than the men's.

Pit toilets

Typical rustic campsite

53

Cell Service

With the park located near Charlevoix cell service is good, which is nice for a rustic park.

Beach and Boating

The park runs six miles along Lake Michigan with parking spots for lake access along the main road. The water is crystal clear and sandy but there are rocks along the shoreline. They are smooth and flat from the many years of waves and sand washing over them.

The park does not have a boat launch.

Shopping and Restaurants

The park does not have a camp store, but is only about 3 miles from Charlevoix. You will find just about anything you could want in Charlevoix including drug stores, grocery stores, fast food restaurants, mom and pop restaurants to fine dining. Downtown Charlevoix has a wonderful shopping district full of shops with souvenirs of all kinds.

Things To Do

Besides hanging out at the beach and rock hunting there are a few miles of hiking trails in the park. The town of Ironton where Lake Charlevoix branched off is about 10 miles away. Here you will find an old historic ferry that transports vehicles and passengers across the narrow part of the lake. I would highly recommend taking a ride on the ferry, but make sure you are not pulling a trailer since the ferry is small.

Lake Michigan shoreline

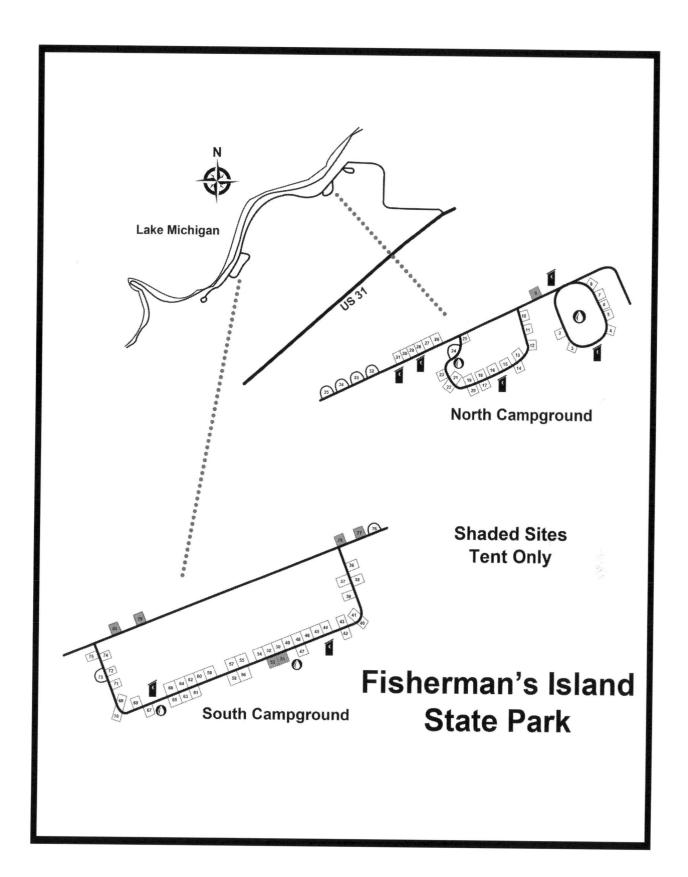

North Campground

Shaded Sites
Tent Only

South Campground

Fisherman's Island
State Park

Otsego Lake State Park

7136 Old 27 S.
Gaylord MI, 49735
989-732-5485

155 campsites
1 mini cabin
62 acres

Semi Modern opens end of April

Modern opens mid May

Modern closes mid October

Semi Modern closes beginning of November

Nestled on the shore of beautiful Otsego Lake is the Otsego Lake State Park. This is a very popular park, close to I-75 with a beautiful beach. It's proximity near Gaylord makes it a nice place to camp if you are interested in staying somewhere that has a variety of stores.

Pros
- Near I-75
- Central location in Northern Michigan
- Near Gaylord
- New bathroom building
- Beautiful beach

Cons
- Small Park at 62 acres
- Near busy road and railroad tracks
- Busy park with lots of day use visitors

Campground

The campground is divided into a north loop and a south loop. The south loop is more popular because it is closer to the lake and has one of the newest bathrooms in the state park system. The north loop is the larger of the two loops, and it has its own little beach with a boardwalk that leads to it. Most sites in both loops are wooded and shady and worn with a dirt surface. There are some small hills in a few areas of the park so you want to make sure you get one that the DNR calls level. The sites on the west side of the park are closer to the water. They are not right on the water, but they are the most popular campsites. Old 27 runs next to the east side of the park and you can hear some road noise. There are also railroad tracks that run between the road and the park. I don't think they are used frequently, but a train did go by during the daytime when I stayed there.

Reservations

Otsego Lake SP is one of the more popular parks. If you want to camp here, you need to make reservations six months to the day. The lots closest to the lake are among the first to be reserved so you have to try to make reservations for them when the system opens at 8 A.M.

North bathroom building

Campsites in south loop

57

South loop bathroom building

Bathrooms

Middle bathroom building

The bathroom in the south loop is one of the nicest bathrooms in the state park system. It's the Taj Mahal of bathrooms. The state must have recived a grant to build this, new, modern environmentally friendly, green building. I would definitely try to get a site in the south loop because of the bathroom building. I stayed in the north so I did not use the new bathroom and I read some reviews that the showers are low pressure and not as warm as people would like because of the green design. The bathroom buildings in the north loop are older buildings but adequate.

Boardwalk to beach in north loop

58

Beach and Boating

The beach on Otsego Lake is nice and sandy with crystal clear water. It's a little bit of a walk from even the closest campsite. There is a large day use parking lot for the beach. During hot weekends it tends to fill up fast and the beach becomes rather crowded. As an alternative you can go down to the north loop and take the boardwalk to the beach. It may be a little less busy.

The park has a nice boat launch with parking for about 40 trucks and trailers. The shoreline along the park is sandy and you can tie your boat up to the shore

Cell Service

I had a good signal and with the campground being near I-75 and Gaylord, I would not expect it to be an issue for most people.

Shopping and Restaurants

The park has a camp store in the beach house that sells necessities and ice cream. Across the street from the entrance to the park is a convenience store that has most of your basic needs. Gaylord is about five miles away and has anything you need with a Meijers and a Walmart to fast food and sit down restaurants.

Things to do

The most popular thing to do at Otsego is to enjoy the beach on a hot sunny day. Fisherman can fish from the fishing pier or use the boat launch if they have a boat. I am not a golfer so I can't give an opinion on how good the golf courses are but there are a few in the Gaylord area. If you are in Gaylord you can check out the elk herd in the City Park located at the end of Grandview Blvd. behind the Secretary of State building.

Beach on Otsego Lake

59

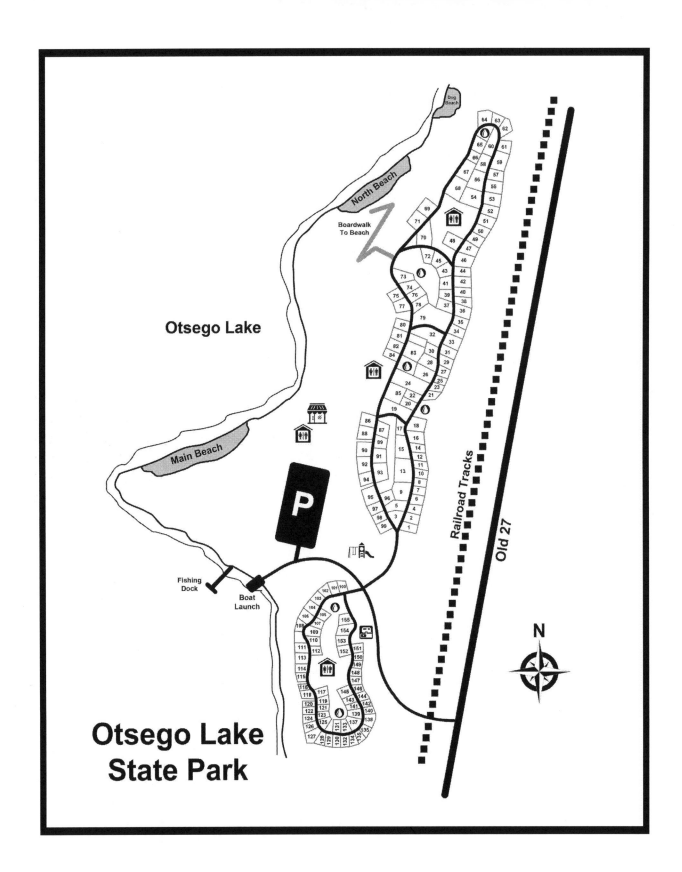

Otsego Lake

Dog Beach

North Beach

Boardwalk
To Beach

Otsego Lake

Main Beach

P

Fishing
Dock

Boat
Launch

Railroad Tracks

Old 27

N

Otsego Lake
State Park

60

Clear Lake State Park

20500 M-33 North
Atlanta MI, 49709
989-785-4388
178 campsites

1 mini cabin
290 acres

Semi modern open all year

Modern opens mid April

Modern closes mid October

Located in the Atlanta State Forest, Clear Lake State Park may only be 200 acres but provides access to hundreds of acres of Michigan forests for hiking, hunting and ORV trails. The park is named after the crystal clear spring fed waters of Clear Lake. It's a secluded and quiet lake with few private houses on its shores.

Pros
- On Clear Lake
- Access to ORV trails
- Beautiful sandy beach

Cons
- Remote location
- Older bathroom buildings

Campground

The campground has 178 campsites which are flat, level and wooded. Most of the campsites have a gravel camping pad. Some sites have a "u" shaped pull through design. The power post is next to the road, so you can pull your trailer parallel to the road and have your awning facing away from the road. The sites in the 200s section are closer to the beach. The sites closest to the water are not directly on the water. They are about 100 feet from the water with trails that lead down to the lake.

Reservations

Because of its remote location, away from any large towns, the park is not as popular as others in northern Michigan. You will still want to get reservations early for holiday weekends. You should be able to if you make reservations in the spring. It is a good choice for last minute getaways because it sometimes has campsites available on weekends.

Campsite at Clear Lake State Park

Bathrooms

Both bathrooms are older but clean since the park is not as busy as other parks in the area. They could use some updating, but it really does not matter which section you camp as far as the bathrooms go.

Clear Lake bathroom building

Beach on Clear Lake

Cell Service

Surprisingly, cell service was really strong for being in such a remote location. I wonder if it is because the DNR has a regional office nearby with a radio tower that has a cell phone antenna added to it. I have AT&T for my provider, but I was told that Verizon does not work well, if you can get a signal at all, while in the park.

Beach and Boating

The beach at Clear Lake S.P. is large and sandy. It's the perfect place to soak up some sun on a hot Michigan day and you can cool off in the clear water of the lake.

The park has a boat launch with a small parking lot. Next to the swimming area the shoreline is sandy so you can pull your boat up to the shore and tie it off.

Shopping and Restaurants

The ranger's station sells firewood and ice, but if you need to go to a larger store you will have to drive to Atlanta which is 10 miles away. Atlanta has a grocery store and a gas station. If you want to go to a bigger town, Alpena is about 50 miles to the east and Gaylord is about 45 miles to the west. There are a few locally owned restaurants in the area. Clear Lake being in such a remote area, I would recommend packing food for meals.

Things To Do

Besides being able to fish, boat, kayak and swim in Clear Lake there are both hiking and ORV trails in the Atlanta State Forest. The ORV trails are near the park, and they will let you ride your ATV in the park from your campsite to the ORV trail. Be sure to verify that with the rangers when you check in as there are some restrictions.

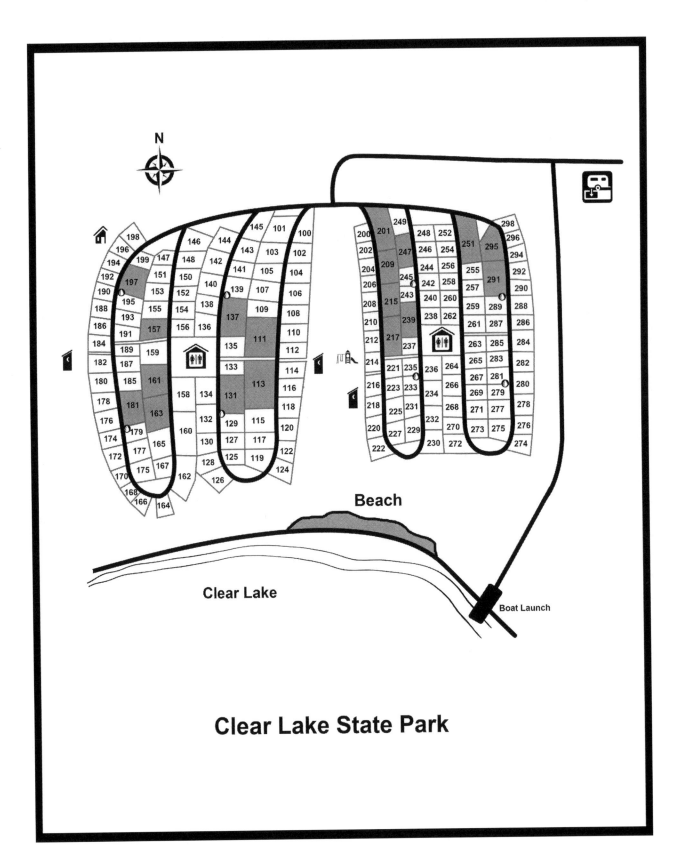

Beach

Clear Lake

Boat Launch

Clear Lake State Park

Leelanau State Park

15310 N. Lighthouse Point Rd.
Northport MI, 49670-9717
231-386-5422

52 rustic campsites
3 mini cabins
1350 acres

Campground Opens end of April

Closes the beginning of November

No modern camping

Many tourists visit Leelanau State Park every year to see the Grand Traverse Lighthouse that stands inside its borders. Not many people stay overnight at the campground because it is rustic only. Located at the tip of the Leelanau Peninsula, it offers stunning views of Lake Michigan and Grand Traverse Bay.

Pros
- Located in Leelanau Peninsula
- Lots of things to do in the area

Cons
- Rustic only campground
- Long trip to the store

Campground

The campground is a rustic campground, and does not have electricity or modern bathrooms. It is right at the tip of the Leelanau Peninsula and has campsites that are right on the water. You can watch the sunrise and sunset while roasting marshmallows at your campfire. The shoreline is rather rocky but accessible. The campsites along the water are open and sunny but the rest of the sites are in the woods and shaded. The sites are all different sizes and shapes along a narrow dirt road. It is more suited to tent camping and smaller trailers. I suppose you could get a large RV to fit if you wanted to, but I am sure you will have some branches scraping along the sides of it as you pull it through the campground. There is no dump station available to empty the gray and black tanks on an RV. I think Interlochen State Park would be the closest state park with a sanitation station. The campground does have a post with a water hose to fill up your freshwater tank.

Reservations

Since it is a rustic campground, It's not very popular with the glamping crowd. You should be able to get a reservation relatively easy.

Leelanau campsite

Shoreline campsite

Lake Michigan shoreline

Bathrooms

It's a rustic campground only pit toilets are available.

Pit toilet at Leelanau

Cell Service

Cell service is weak so you may or may not have service depending on your location in the park

Beach and Boating

There is no boat launch and not much of a beach. The shoreline is rocky which is perfect for rock hunting but not so much if you want to build sand castles and lay out on a beach. Dogs are not allowed on the beach in order to protect the Piping Plover habitat.

Shopping and Restaurants

If you need to get any necessities, Northport is about 10 miles away. Like most of the towns in the Leelanau Peninsula, it's a small town and mostly caters to the tourists. If you need to go to a big town, Traverse City is about an hour away since the drive there is mostly winding two lane road.

Things To Do

The highlight of Leelanau State Park is all the things to do in the area. The Leelanau Peninsula is one of the most popular tourist destinations in the Midwest. You can check out the lighthouse or hike the miles of trails near Mud Lake, both are part of the park. Not too far away is the Sleeping Bear Dunes National Lakeshore. Leeland and historic Fishtown are nearby. There are also plenty of small towns like Glen Arbor or Suttons Bay that offer tourists shopping and dining to fit any budget. If you are feeling lucky you can stop by the Leelanau Sands Casino. There is so much to see and do in the Leelanau Peninsula that you could travel around it for a month and not see or do it all.

Grand Traverse Lighthouse

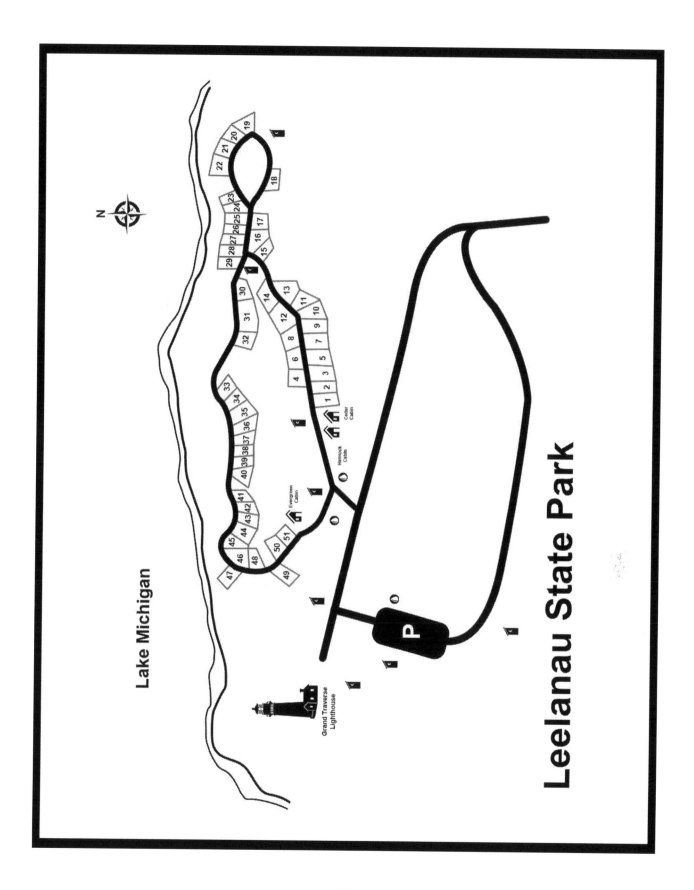

Lake Michigan

Grand Traverse
Lighthouse

Hemlock
Cabin

Evergreen
Cabin

Cedar
Cabin

Leelanau State Park

Keith J. Charters State Park

1132 US-31 N.
Traverse City MI, 49686
231-922-5270

343 Campsites
1 cottage
2 mini cabins
47 acres

A section of the campground and one modern bathroom are open all year.

Campground opens mid May

Campground closes mid October

Keith J Charters Traverse City State Park is about 2 miles from Downtown Traverse City making it a popular tourist destination. Back in the 1920s it was a quiet location, but as the city grew around the park it became a much needed public park butt a busy one. At 343 campsites on 47 acres it's mostly campground with a stretch of beach on Grand Traverse Bay

Pros
- Near downtown Traverse City
- Year round camping
- Wooded sites
- Bike path to downtown

Cons
- Near downtown Traverse City
- Lots of noise from road and airport
- Difficult to exit park due to traffic

Campground

The campground is flat and heavily wooded. It is well used and the sites are mostly dirt with little grass. With US-31 running next to the campground it's best to be in the back far away from the road where it is less noisy. Cherry Capital Airport is not far from the park so you will hear the planes taking off and landing. If you have a trailer, the noise won't be as noticeable, but if you are camping in a tent or pop-up you will remember your stay at Traverse City with all the noise. It is definitely worth staying at the campground with its close proximity to downtown Traverse City. In a town where a cheap motel is about $150 a night, the cost to stay at the State Park is a bargain. If you are looking for a quieter campground to stay at or if Traverse City is full, check out Interlochen State Park.

Reservations

With Traverse City being a popular tourist destination, the park is also a popular place to stay at. You will want to get reservations six months to the day for holidays, and especially for the Cherry Festival during the Fourth Of July week.

Campground

Bathrooms

Each of the three bathrooms in the campground are different. The bathroom furthest away from the entrance, near site 250, is the newest building. It's a brick building with a row of showers across from the bathrooms. The other two bathroom buildings are older and of wood construction. The park gets a lot of use and so do the bathrooms. The staff does their best to keep them clean, but it is a busy park.

Bathroom building near site 230

Bathroom building near site 212

Bathroom building near site 250

Cell Service

This is the one campground I can say, for sure, that you will most likely have good phone service since it is in the largest city in the northern Lower Peninsula.

Beach and Boating

The park has a large sandy beach on Grand Traverse Bay. The problem is that it's on the other side of US-31, one of the busiest roads in northern Michigan. An overhead walkway takes pedestrians over the traffic from the campground to the beach. It can be difficult to haul a wagon or a lot of beach gear over the walkway, but it's safer and easier than crossing the road. The beach does have a large parking lot, but it usually has a lot of day use visitors. A beach house with modern toilets is available for sunbathers to use along with a new playground for the kids. Considering the price people are paying to stay in a hotel on the bay, it's a great deal to stay at the campground instead and walk over to the beach.

Walkway overpass to beach

Beach on Grand Traverse Bay

72

Playscape at the beach

Shopping and Restaurants

When it comes to shopping near Traverse City State Park you will find just about anything, from small artsy gift shops to big box stores and shopping malls. You can get just about any kind of food, from fast food to brew pubs and fine dining. Traverse City is a foodies paradise. Most everything is nearby but the biggest challenge is the traffic, especially through downtown. One thing I have learned is to take a right turn out of the park and go down to North Four Mile road and then go around to Airport Road to get over to Walmart, Meijer and the mall.

Things To Do

There is a never ending list of things to do in the Traverse City area. You can go exploring downtown to wine tasting at the wineries in Old Mission Point or even venturing out to the Leelanau Peninsula and Sleeping Bear Dunes. Be sure to visit the old state hospital that has been renovated into housing and shops known as The Village at Grand Traverse Commons. If you have bicycles, a paved rail trail that runs right behind the campground will take you downtown so you can avoid the traffic. If relaxing at the campsite or on the beach is not enough, you can always find something to do while staying in Traverse City.

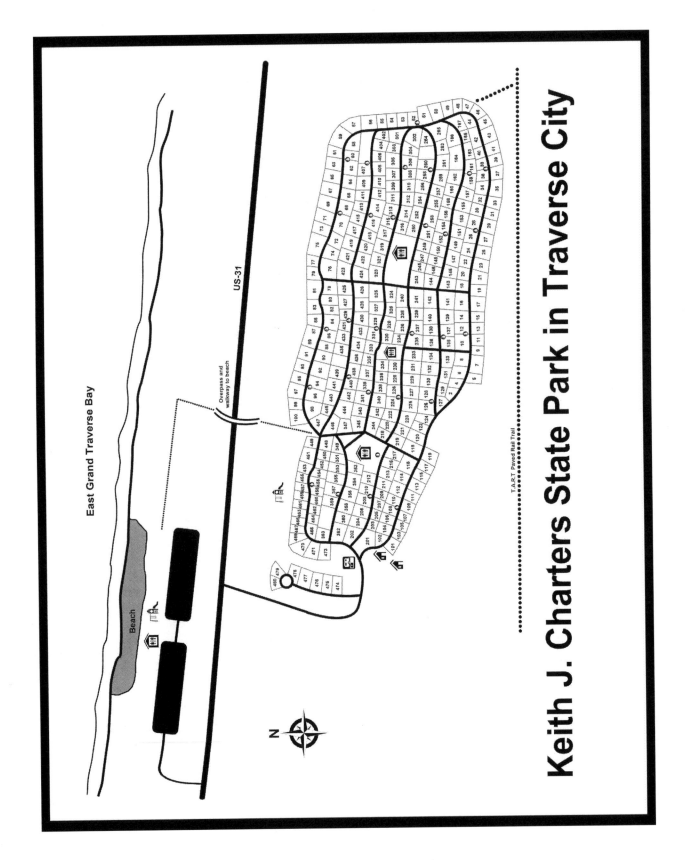

Keith J. Charters State Park in Traverse City

East Grand Traverse Bay

Beach

US-31

Overpass and
walkway to beach

T.A.R.T Paved Rail Trail

Interlochen State Park

4167 M-137
Interlochen MI, 49643
231-276-9511

392 modern campsites
52 rustic campsites
3 mini cabins
187 acres

Campgrounds open the end of April

Campgrounds close end of October

Interlochen State Park is the largest park in the system in terms of total number of campsites, with almost 500. When the park is full there are so many people that it feels like a small city. It's location near Traverse City and the Leelanau Peninsula makes it a great location with lots of stuff to do.

Pros
- Near Traverse City
- Has some pull through sites
- Across from Interlochen Center for the Arts
- Located near Sleeping Bear Dunes

Cons
- Large Park with lots of people
- Possible swimmers itch in lake

Campground

The modern part of the campground is divided into two loops, a north loop and a south loop. When I was there the north loop was more popular. The sites in that section seemed a little bigger and more accommodating to larger rigs. The southern loop itself is larger and has a lot of campsites. One drawback to the southern loop is the large valley that runs through the middle of the campground. The sites are "stair stepped" Making them somewhat level, but I don't recommend this area. The campsites have trees throughout but, they are heavily wooded. You will have to check the DNR website to see if the site you want is shaded or not. There is a boat launch in the south loop, which is popular with kayakers and fishermen. My first choice to camp at would be the north side but both sides offer a nice place to stay and relax.

On the other side of the road from the modern campground is the Green Lake Rustic Campground. It is what you would expect for a rustic campground with smaller tent sites and trees. It also has the typical pit toilets. If you don't mind the primitive bathrooms it is a nice and quiet campground that overlooks Green Lake.

North campground

Reservations

Reservations for Interlochen are usually easy to get since the campground has so many sites. The sites along the lake are the most popular and you should reserve those as soon as you can. I would also make reservations as early as possible for holiday weekends. The most popular weekend is the Fourth of July since the Cherry Festival is happening in Traverse City. For the most part, this is a good park to check for last minute campsites as they may have some available since there are so many campsites.

South campground

Bathrooms

The two bathrooms in the north side are identical brick buildings. They are much newer than the bathrooms in the south side of the park. Another reason why the north loop is more popular.

The bathrooms in the south loop are older but well maintained. Don't let them deter you from staying at Interlochen

Bathroom in south campground near site 492

Bathroom in south campground near site 475

Bathroom building in North campground

Cell Service

I had decent cell service at Interlochen State Park. It was not really strong and video was slow, but it worked for texting and basic internet.

Beaches and Boating

There is a nice sandy beach at Interlochen on Duck Lake, between the north and south loops. I was there in the middle of the week and it was not too crowded but when the park is full the beach could be crowded. If you like to be near the beach I would recommend the sites in the north loop. The sites closest to the beach in the south loop are not totally level. There was a sign posted with a warning about swimmers itch. I have not read any online complaints about it as I have for Higgins Lake, but I would take precautions such as showering immediately after swimming.

Playground at beach on Duck Lake

Beach on Duck Lake

Beach house at beach on Duck Lake

78

Shopping and Restaurants

The park does have a camp store in the beach house. It has basic necessities and a small concession stand. Interlochen is not a large town, but there is a nice size grocery store about 2 miles from the campground. There is also a gas to fuel up at after towing a big heavy trailer. If you don't feel like cooking, Bud's is about a mile from the campground. The food is excellent and they also have a gift shop. About 10 miles away at Chums Corner, the intersection of M-31 and M-37 is just about any store you can think of. If you need something it is only about 10 minutes away.

Things To Do

I think Interlochen S.P. is a great place to stay for a week or even longer since there is so much to do in the area. It's between Traverse City and Sleeping Bear Dunes. You could also go shopping in downtown Frankfort and visit the lighthouse there. If you like lighthouses you are not far from Point Betsie, Grand Traverse Lighthouse and Old Mission Point Lighthouse. The Music school is right across the street if you want to listen to a concert check their schedule. They have some performances by the teachers that you can listen to for free and some big name artists, but you will need tickets to listen to their concerts.

Playground in south campground

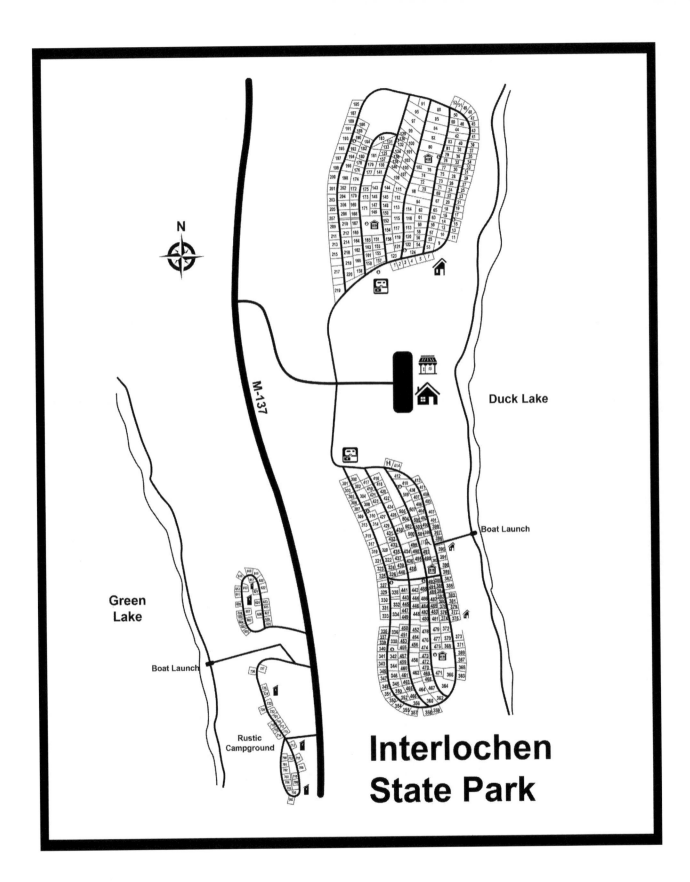

N

M-137

Duck Lake

Green
Lake

Boat Launch

Boat Launch

Rustic
Campground

Interlochen
State Park

Hartwick Pines State Park

4216 Ranger Road
Grayling MI, 49738
989-348-7068

100 campsites
1 cabin
9762 acres

Semi Modern opens beginning of April

Modern opens the end of April

Modern closes mid October

Semi modern closes early December

Established in the 20s, the park was donated to the state by Karen Hartwick in memory of her husband Edward E. Hartwick, a lumberman who was killed in World War I. Conveniently located off I-75 near Grayling Hartwick State Park is the 3rd largest state park in the Lower Peninsula. It is the home to the Hartwick Pines Logging Museum where tourists can experience what it was like to be a lumberjack in the 19th century.

Pros
- Located near Grayling
- A lot of hiking and biking trails
- Logging Museum
- Full Hookup Sites

Cons
- No beach
- No cell service

Campground

The campground at Hartwick Pines has 100 campsites. About 40 of them are full hookup pull-through sites with water, electricity and sewer, which is rare for most state parks. All of the campsites have at least 30 amp electricity. The campground is flat and all sites have a paved pad to park your RV or trailer on. The sites with full hookup have small trees and are in full sun. Sites 20 to 60 are heavily wooded. Some are cut into individually pocketed sites within the trees, and are ideal for tent camping. Be sure to look at the site descriptions when making reservations.

Wooded campsite

Reservations

The full hookup sites are very popular and you will need to make reservations six months to the day. Because of the lack of a beach the campground is not as popular as some of the other parks in the area such as Otsego. Other than holiday weekends or during the peak of the Autumn color, you probably can get last minute reservations here.

Pull through full hook-up site

82

Bathrooms

The campground has only one bathroom. It's an older building but it was updated when the full hookup sites were created. It's located in the center of the campground and the sites on the outside can be a long walk to the bathroom.

Cell Service

Cell service is non existent in the park. I could not make phone calls or text, let alone get data to work. Plan on going into or near Grayling to get contact with the outside world.

Bathroom building

Beach and Boating

Hartwick does not have a beach although it does have four small lakes within its boundaries. They have a muddy seaweed bottom and are not suitable for swimming. They are ideal for canoeing and kayaking. Boats with motors are prohibited on the lakes. The Michigan DNR stocks the ponds with trout and a trout stamp is required to fish in them.

Bright Lake public access

Shopping and Restaurants

Hartwick Pines State Park is about 6 miles from Grayling. You will find just about anything you need in Grayling from grocery and hardware stores to fast food and sit down restaurants.

Things To Do

Even though the park does not have a beach there is plenty to do at Hartwick Pines. You can hike the many miles of trails. The campground has a nice playscape for the kids to burn off a little energy. You can visit the nature center or logging museum. The Chapel in the Woods is not to be missed while you are at the park. You can fish one of the lakes. Both Glory Lake and Bright Lake have fishing docks. A paved bike path runs from the park to Grayling. The park is open year round and offers hunting in the fall and cross country skiing in the winter.

The Hartwick Pines Chapel

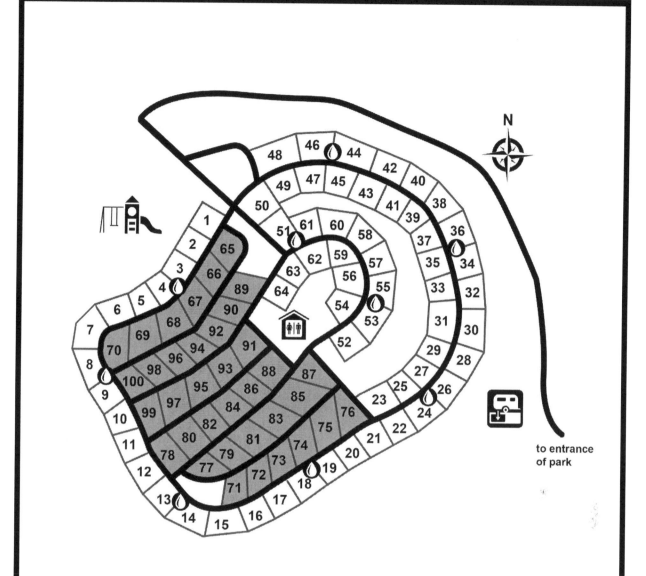

Hartwick Pines State Park
Campground

Shaded sites are full hookup

North Higgins State Park

11747 N. Higgins Lake Drive
Roscommon MI, 48653
989-821-6125

174 campsites
2 mini cabins
449 acres

Semi Modern open all year
Modern opens mid April
Modern closes mid October

North Higgins State Park is located in the most logical place, on the north side of Higgins Lake. The 449 acre park was constructed on what used to be the world's largest seedling nursery. With it's large sandy beach and a bike path that runs through the park it's a wonderful place to enjoy Michigan's outdoors.

Pros
- Between I-75 and US-127
- Large Beach
- Paved bike path

Cons
- Long drive to store
- Long walk to the beach

Campground

The campground is divided into an east and a west campground. The west campground is the more popular of the two, with tall shade trees and newer bathroom building. The sites are level, but are usually dirt and gravel because they see more use. The east side has fewer trees and is more open and sunny. Some of the lesser used sites are more grass covered. The bathroom is older and sits on top of a hill. You will have to climb stairs or go up a hill on the road to access it. Because of the hill some of the sites near the bathroom are less likely to be level.

It does not matter what side you are camping at, it will be a long walk to the beach. It's located between the two sides. I do think the east side is a little closer since the boat ramp is between the west side and the beach.

West campground

Reservations

The park is a popular destination with its proximity to two major expressways so you will want to make reservations as soon as you can. For holidays you will need to make your reservations six months to the day.

Bathrooms

The bathroom in the west side is a newer brick building and typical layout with showers on one side and bathrooms on the other side of a hallway. The bathroom on the east side is an older wooden structure. It's been updated but not as nice as the west side.

East campground bathroom building

West campground bathroom building

Cell Service

I had a couple of bars of service but it was not strong. It would be sufficient for texts and phone calls but not great for streaming videos of your favorite sporting events.

Beach and Boating

The beach is a large sandy beach stretching along Higgins Lake. You should have plenty of room to lay out in the sun. There are also a few trees along the shore so you can find some shade if you want to get out of the hot sunlight. The shoreline has grills and picnic tables for guests to use. Higgins Lake is known for swimmers itch and the campground has an outdoor shower near the beach house so you can rinse off after getting out of the water.

The park has a boat launch. It's not as nice as South Higgins S.P. but it does have a large parking lot. Be aware that the number of boats on the lake is limited and when they reach the limit you will not be allowed to launch your boat.

Beach house

Beach shower

Beach on Higgins Lake

Shopping and Restaurants

About a mile east of the park is a gas station with a Dairy Queen so you can fill up your tank and your tummy. A couple miles to the west, down Old 127 is a small grocery store and a pizza place. If you need to go to the big city to a large store or have a craving for fast food Grayling is about 12 miles away. It does not take too long to get there on the expressway with a speed limit of 75 mph.

Things To Do

If you want to do more that just lay on the beach or boat and fish on Higgins Lake, There is about 10 miles of hiking trails to explore across the street from the park. The trails are available for hiking, cross-country skiing and biking. You can also visit the Higgins Lake Nursery and CCC Museum which is near the park.

Paved bike path

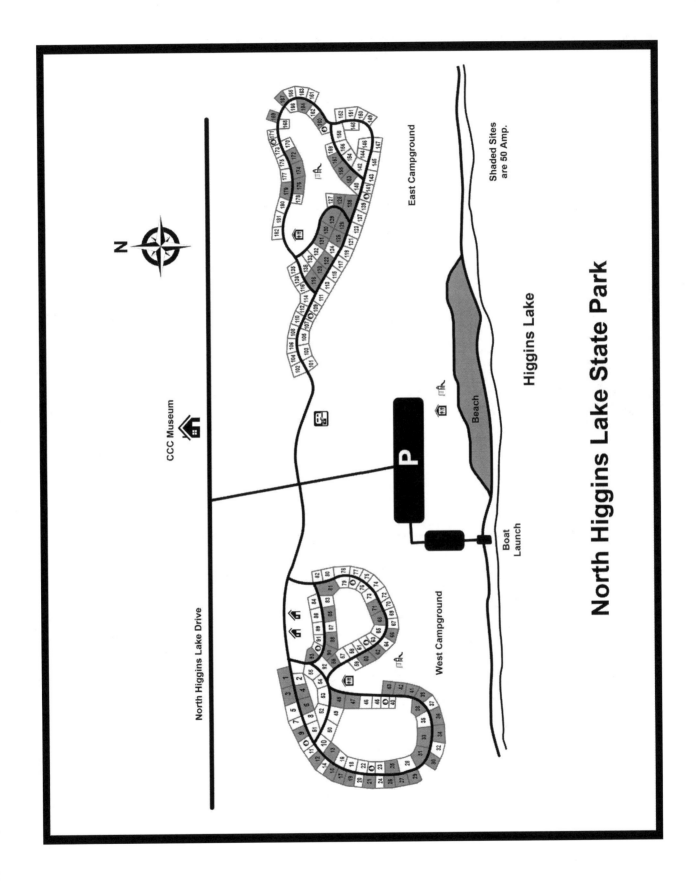

North Higgins Lake State Park

South Higgins State Park

106 State Park Drive
Roscommon MI, 48653
989-821-6374

400 campsites
1 mini cabin
1000 acres

Modern campground opens Mid April

Modern campground closes beginning
of December

No semi modern camping

Located along the southern shore of Higgins
Lake is appropriately named South Higgins
Lake State Park. It's an extremely popular and
busy state park with over 300 campsites and a
natural harbor at the boat launch.

Pros
- Located between I-75 and US-127
- Natural harbor for parking boats
- Small lake and hiking across the street

Cons
- Popular park and usually crowded
- Shopping can be a long drive

Campground

The campground is large with over 300 campsites. It's popular and usually full and that's why most sites are worn down to dirt. The sites closer to the lake are more open and full sun. The farther away you get from the lake the more wooded the sites are. The east part of the campground is the most popular section especially with boaters since it's near the lagoon where you can beach your boat and tie it up. The south west part of the campground has somewhat of a hill. I would avoid that part if you can but the sites are "stair stepped" so they will be kind of level. It is a busy park and there will be a lot of people camping along with you. Some people have given the park the unofficial designation of the "party campground." Over the years the park has been more diligent about enforcing the rules.

Bathroom building near site 39

One of three brick bathroom buildings

Campground away from lake

Campground near lake

Reservations

South Higgins is a popular park and you will need to make reservations six months to the day for weekends in the summer.

Bathrooms

The bathroom on the east side is the oldest bathroom in the campground. I guess that is the downside of staying on the east side. It's not a bad bathroom it's just older than the other three bathrooms in the campground. The other three are all identical brick buildings, and the common style with showers on the end.

Cell Service

Cell service was OK with a couple of bars, but I would not expect it to be great since the park is rather far from any large cities.

Beach and Boating

The designated beach area is at the east end of the park, on the other side of the boat ramp from the campground. It's a beautiful sandy beach with a log cabin style beach house built by the CCC camps. There is sand all along the shoreline in the campground for lake access if you don't want to make the trip to the beach. Please note that swimmers itch is prevalent in Higgins Lake and you are advised to rinse off after exiting the water.

Day use beach on Higgins Lake

The boat ramp and facilities are probably the best in the state park system. With three launches together and a large parking lot the park can accommodate a large number of boaters. Be aware that there is a limit on how many boats can be on Lake Higgins at any time and they do count the number of boats coming into the park. When the limit is reached you will not be allowed to launch your boat. The boat launch is in a small natural harbor with sandy banks that allows boaters to tie up their boats on the shoreline. This is why Higgins South is so popular with boaters.

Beach house and camp store

Boat lagoon

Shopping and Restaurants

Besides the camp store next to the beach, you can go about a mile west of the entrance where you will find an ice cream store, pizza place, party store and a gas station. If you need something that the local places do not have, it's about a 20 minute drive to Prudenville where you will find big chain drug stores, a Walmart and a hardware store.

Things To Do

Besides swimming and boating on Higgins Lake, across the road from the main entrance is access to Marl Lake for fishing or kayaking. About 7 miles of hiking trails wind their way around this little lake. If it's raining out and you want something to do, check out the Pines Theater between Prudenville and Houghton Lake, it's a historic theater in a log cabin. The Houghton Lake area also offers golf and miniature golf along with some antique shopping if you are looking for ways to spend some money.

Playground near campground beach

Four hole dump station

94

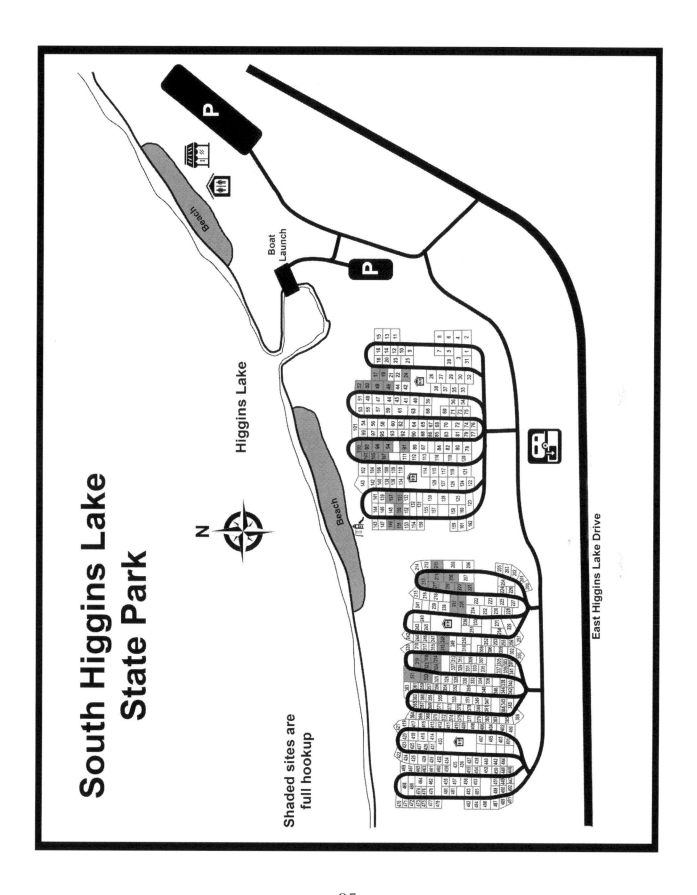

South Higgins Lake State Park

Beach

Higgins Lake

Boat Launch

N

Beach

Shaded sites are full hookup

East Higgins Lake Drive

95

Mitchell State Park

6093 E. M-115
Cadillac MI, 49601
231-775-7911

221 campsites
2 mini cabins

Campground and modern bathroom building open all year

Located between Lake Mitchell and Lake Cadillac, near the intersection of M-55 and M-115, in the center of the mitten it is a great place for a getaway. The park is extremely popular with anglers looking to catch the "big one" with two lakes to fish and a canal between them to tie your boat up.

Pros
- Between Lake Cadillac and Lake Mitchell
- Excellent park for fishermen
- Near Cadillac

Cons
- Road noise from M-115
- Not a lot of Shade
- Main beach on other side of road

Campground

The campground is large and flat. It's not heavily wooded but there are some large trees providing some shade. The north side, near the canal, is the most popular part of the campground. Campers with boats like being able to tie up their boat up to the side of the canal and they covet the nearby campsites. Most of the campsites have a gravel camping pad, be sure to check the site descriptions to see if the one you want is gravel or dirt.

M-115 runs along the west side of the campground. For that reason I would recommend being as far to the east side as possible in order to avoid the noise of the constant traffic. Lake Cadillac is on the east side and the sites at the ends of the loops have a good view of the lake but are not directly on the lake. The shoreline has large rocks and boulders for protection against erosion and is not ideal for swimming with the exception of a small beach at the south end of the campground. A fishing dock extends into the lake if you want to do some fishing and don't have a boat.

Mitchell State Park Campground

Reservations

For holiday weekends you are going to want to make your reservations six months to the day. If you want one of the prized campsites along the canal you will need to make those early as well. For the other sites you can probably find availability in the spring for summer weekends but I would still make reservations as soon as you can.

Bathrooms

The campground has two bathroom buildings. The bathroom in the southeast corner is an older wooden structure. The bathroom in the northwest corner is newer and more common style brick structure. The brick one is the nicer of the two bathrooms.

Southeast bathroom building

Northwest bathroom building

Beach and Boating

The park has two boat launches. One is on Lake Mitchell in the day use area and has parking for trailers. The other on Lake Cadillac in the north east corner, is mainly for campers since there is no parking available. If you are lucky, you might find a place along the canal to tie up your boat. It can be busy with a lot of boaters in the summer.

The park also has two beaches. The main beach is on Lake Mitchell, west of M-115. If you are camping, instead of crossing the busy road, you can access the beach by using the walkway next to the canal that goes under the bridge.

The other beach, for people staying in the campground, is located at the south end of the park on Lake Cadillac. It's a small beach but it is a nice spot if you don't want to walk all the way over to the main beach.

Cell Service

I had two bars of cell service, being near the town of Cadillac, I would expect you will have fairly good service.

Day use beach on Lake Mitchell

Canal between Lake Mitchell and Lake Cadillac

Shopping and Restaurants

The area near the park has a lot of fast food places, restaurants, gas stations and party stores. The campground is walking distance to most of these places which is a good thing since pulling out of the park onto M-115 can be a challenge because of the heavy traffic. If you don't want to cook, Burger King, Subway and McDonald's are right next to the campground. If you want to go into the big city of Cadillac it's only about 5 miles away on the other end of Lake Cadillac and is a quick trip from the park.

Things To Do

The campground has a nice playscape next to Lake Cadillac for the kids. If you don't have a boat and you want to take a break from relaxing on the beach, you can hike the miles of trails and look for wildlife at the Cadillac Heritage Nature Study Area on the north side of the canal. Next to the campground is the Carl T. Johnson Hunting and Fishing Center. The center includes both archery and pellet gun ranges and offers scheduled shooting programs throughout the summer. An exhibit hall displays the rise of sportsmen and sportswomen and their contributions to more than 150 years of Michigan history. There is also a miniature golf and go kart track about a mile north of the park if you want to race your kids or practice your putting like Happy Gilmore.

Fishing dock on Lake Cadillac

Playground in campground near Lake Cadillac

99

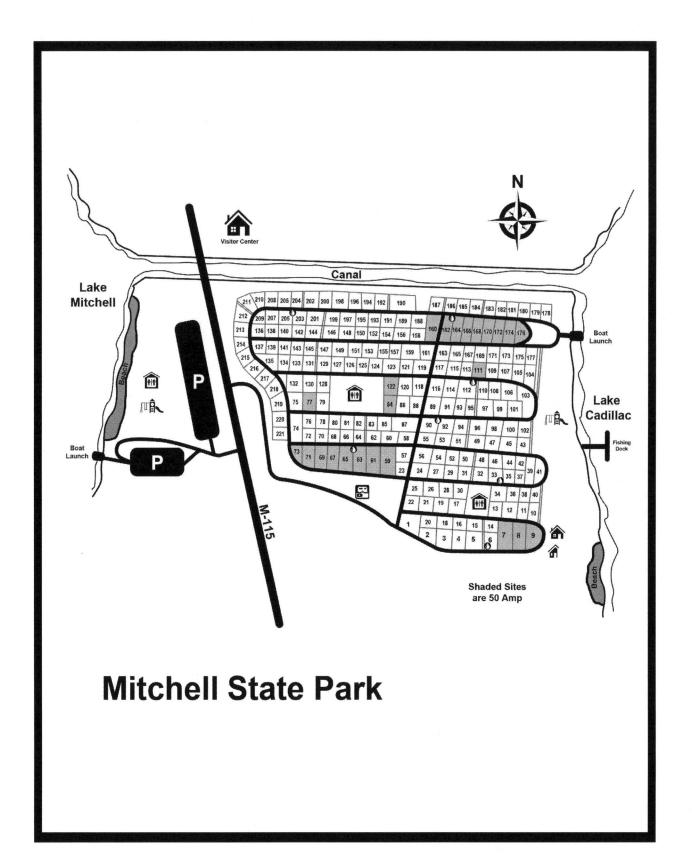

Mitchell State Park

Wilson State Park

910 N. First Street
Harrison MI, 48625
989-539-3021

158 campsites
1 lodge
36 acres

Modern opens beginning of May

Modern closes end of November

No semi modern camping

Located in the small town of Harrison, on Budd Lake, Wilson State Park is popular with Michiganians who live in the central Lower Peninsula. It's not a large park but with its sandy beach and easy access to US-127 it's a nice place to stay for a weekend. The buildings in the park are older, but they have been well maintained. The park was originally the site of the Wilson Brothers Sawmill and Company Store, which thrived in the late 1800s. The company donated the land to the city of Harrison, which in turn donated it to the state. The 36 acre park was created in 1927.

Pros
- Located in central Michigan
- Shopping nearby
- Nice little beach

Cons
- Next to noisy road
- Small park with few activities

Campground

The campground is split into a north and a south loop. The north loop is relatively flat except for the north west corner around site 40. There is a little bit of a hill but it's not too bad. The south loop is rather hilly, especially in the back corner in the area around site 125. Both sides have numerous trees and are shady. The biggest issue with the campground is it's proximity to Old US-127 and the noise from the traffic. The sites near the road are only a few feet away an the traffic going in and out of town is heavy. You will want to be as far away from the road as possible. The Clare County Fairgrounds are directly across the street from the state park. You will probably want to check their schedule to decide if you want to stay during the fair or an activity happening at the fairgrounds. I have been told that theft is an issue at Wilson State Park so make sure to lock everything up at night and especially if your site will be left unattended for any length of time. I would recommend this wherever you stay. I think it is uncommon but unfortunately it does happen.

Reservations

Because of the road noise it's not a popular park but I would recommend booking as early as you can for holiday weekends. It is a good option for getting last minute reservations.

Bathrooms

Both bathrooms are older wooden construction but well maintained. With the two of them being a similar layout and construction the bathrooms are not a deciding factor in whichever loop you decide to camp in.

One of two identical bathroom buildings

Wilson State Park campground

Cell Service

Because the state park is basically in the town of Harrison cell service is good and should be rather reliable.

Beach and Boating

The beach is rather unique with an upper and a lower section. A 6 foot tall stone wall holds sand with a stairway going down to a lower beach at the water's edge. I assume this was done because the beach would have been too steep. The park has a nice older stone and log beach house and pavilion.

Wilson State Park does not have a boat launch. A county boat launch is at the south end of Budd Lake. Also note that the lake is " slow, no wake" from 6 pm at night to 10 am the following morning.

Shopping and Restaurants

The park is basically in the middle of the town of Harrison. There are grocery stores, gas stations, a hardware store and a McDonalds. You could easily walk to many places in about 10 minutes if you wanted to. A sidewalk runs next to the park along Business 127 and through town.

Historic beach house

Things To Do

Budd Lake is a nice little lake to enjoy while staying at Wilson S.P. The park is small and does not have any hiking trails or any nearby state land to enjoy. Harrison is a nice town, but I would not consider it to be a tourist town like Boyne City or Traverse City area. There is a go-kart and miniature golf place in town. If you want a place to hang out, relax at your campsite and go to the beach, Wilson is perfect for that. If you plan to stay for a week and are looking for lots of stuff to do you will probably be disappointed.

Beach on Budd Lake

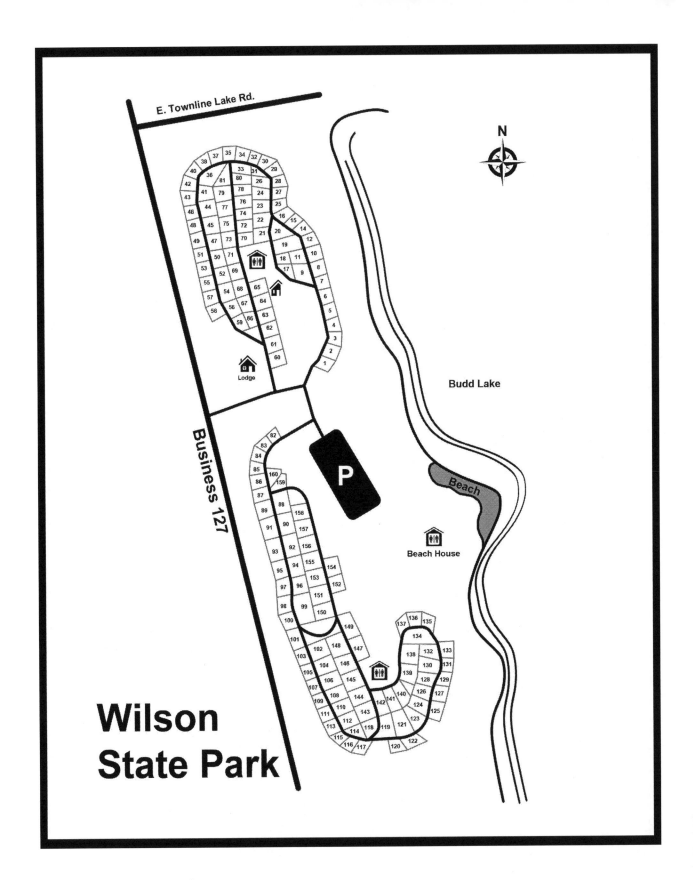

E. Townline Lake Rd.

N

Budd Lake

Beach

Beach House

P

Lodge

Business 127

Wilson
State Park

Orchard Beach State Park

2064 N. Lakeshore Road
Manistee MI, 49660
231-723-7422

166 campsites
1 cabin
201 acres

Modern campground opens mid April

Modern campground closes late October

Semi-modern camping not available

With a name like Orchard Beach you would expect the park to have a beach but unfortunately years of erosion and high water levels have claimed it. In the late 1800s, George Hart cleared the land where the park is now and planted an apple orchard, which gave the park its name. He ran a trolley line from Manistee for people to visit his farm. In 1921, the state purchased the farm and built a campground among the apple trees. If you don't mind staying at a park without a beach, then Orchard Beach State Park is a great option. With full hookup sites and located near Manistee, it is a great location on the west coast of Michigan.

Pros
- Near Manistee
- Full hookup sites
- On northwest side of state

Cons
- No Beach
- Small state park

Campground

The campground is a smaller one with only 166 campsites. It's sparsely wooded with some tall trees for shade but you can still expect to have plenty of sunshine on a sunny day. The campground is mostly flat and level with paved roads and most sites have gravel camping pads. I would avoid staying on the campsites near M-110 as they are only about 30 feet from the road. If you can get a site in the back loop near the lake, those are probably the best sites since you can get a good view of the lake and the evening sunsets.

Reservations

Reservations for campsites are somewhat easy to get. Since the park does not have a beach it is not that popular. Campsites for summer can usually be reserved in the spring or even last minute.

Cell Service

Cell service was reasonably strong at the park. Located near Manistee you can expect to get a decent signal

Bathrooms

The park has two bathroom buildings and one beach house. They were all built by the CCC camps during the Depression in the 30s. They are not new but have been updated since they were constructed.

The bathroom building near the entrance and the ranger station is an oddly shaped building but it does have bathrooms and showers

The main bathroom building is near the center of the campground, on the east side, near the road. It is a unique old historic building with stone walls, but it has modern toilets and showers.

The beach house has bathrooms inside it. Even though it is a short walk to the beach house it can be difficult for some to reach since you have to walk up a hill. I find it odd to call it a beach house since there is no longer a beach at the park.

Orchard Beach campground

Main Bathroom Building near center of Campground

Bathroom building near the entrance

Beach and Boating

Unfortunately, a park named Orchard Beach does not have a beach. Looking at the map you would think there would be a beach since it is near Lake Michigan, but there is a hundred foot drop to the water. A set of stairs descends to the water, but they have been closed because of the erosion. If you want to go to a beach, 5th Avenue Beach and Douglas Park in Manistee are only a few miles away. Because the park is on top of a cliff, it does not have a boat launch.

Shopping and Restaurants

The park does not have a camp store but Manistee is only a few miles away and has grocery stores, gas stations and drug stores. The downtown area has some nice little shops and restaurants to explore. South of town are some of your favorite fast food chains like McDonalds, Wendy's and Taco Bell. Well, maybe they are not your favorite, but they are there for a quick meal.

Things To Do

Across the road from the campground is 2.5 miles of hiking trails. If you want to try to win it big, the Little River Casino is only a few miles away. The town of Manistee has a lot of historic buildings to see and you can tour the museum ship S.S. City Of Milwaukee. The campground may not have a beach but there is plenty to see and do in the area and you are not too far from the Sleeping Bear Dunes National Lakeshore.

Stairway to lake closed to public

Beach house

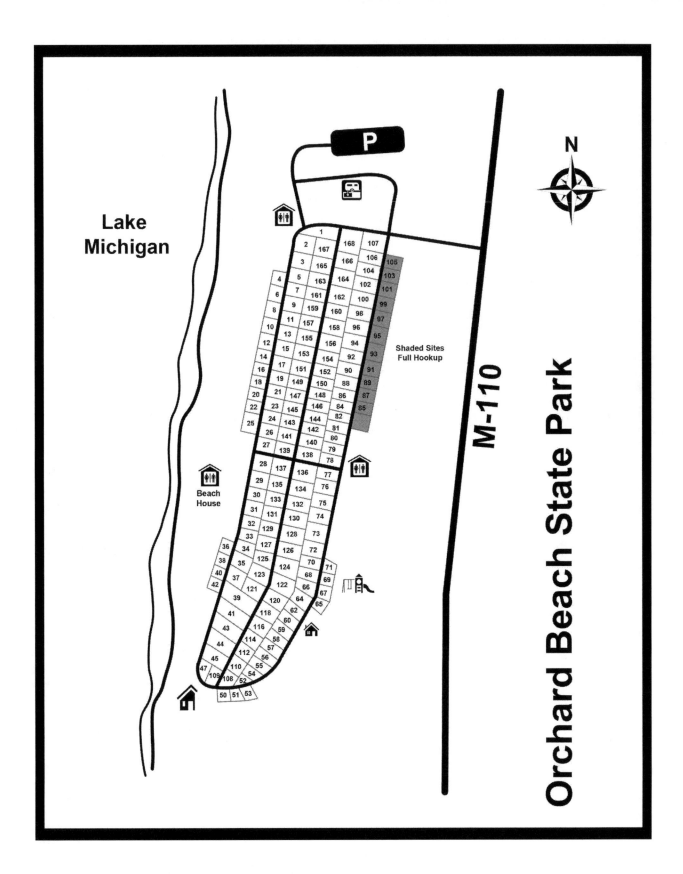

Lake
Michigan

P

Shaded Sites
Full Hookup

M-110

Beach
House

Orchard Beach State Park

108

Ludington State Park

8800 W. M-116
Ludington MI, 49431
231-843-2423

352 modern sites
10 hike in sites
3 mini cabins
5300 acres

Semi modern open all year

Modern opens end of March

Modern closes end of October

If you ask anyone that has ever camped at Ludington State Park what their favorite park in Michigan is, they will probably tell you Ludington. It is one of the most popular state parks and for good reason. With miles of shoreline along Lake Michigan, an inland lake, miles of hiking trails and located near the tourist town of Ludington there is a lot to love about it.

Pros
- Nature lovers paradise
- Beautiful sandy beach
- Near Ludington

Cons
- Nearly impossible to get reservations
- Busy park with lots of people

Campground

The campground is divided into three modern campgrounds. The sites in all three of the campgrounds tend to be small because I think they are trying to accommodate as many campers as they can. Each campground has one bathroom with a walk up sewer for dumping your portable blue crap wagon if you have one. The sanitation station is about a half mile down the road from all three campgrounds.

Pines Campground

The Pines is the closest to Lake Michigan. It has plenty of tall trees and most of the sites are shaded. The front half of the campground is flat and the back half is a little hilly. Some sites have paved camping pads, some have grass and the sites towards the lake are a little sandy. Even though the Pines is closest to the Lake Michigan beach, it is still a little bit of a walk since there is a large parking lot to cross before you get there. From the back of the campground to the beach I would say it's about a quarter mile walk.

Cedar Campground

This is the smallest of the three campgrounds. It has few trees and mostly is open sun. The lots have some grass, but I am sure it is difficult for the grass to grow well since the sites see a lot of use all summer long. It is the farthest away from either beach in the park. Since it is such a long walk, you may want to drive to the beach.

Beechwood Campground

Closest to Lake Hamlin, this campground is heavily wooded with lots of shade. It also has some hills and small sites so be sure to check the site description when making reservations. Beechwood is closest to the beach and playground on Hamlin Lake but it is still a long walk to the beach even from the closest campsites.

Jack Pines Campground

For hikers, the Jack Pines Campground provides a quiet place to pitch a tent. It's a rustic campground only accessible to hikers. It has a hand pump for water and some pit toilets. I guess that's the inconvenience of getting some peace and quiet in a secluded campground.

Pines Campground

Cedar Campground

Reservations

Reservations for Ludington are almost impossible to acquire. You will have to try to make them six months to the day, first thing in the morning when the system turns on for the day. You probably won't be able to chose a specific site, you will more than likely have to take whatever is available. Hopefully your trailer will fit, It is very important to check the dimensions of the site.

Bathrooms

The bathrooms at Ludington are all brick construction and older buildings. They have been updated, however they do get a lot of use. The bathroom in the Cedar Campground is probably the best bathroom building, but it is nothing spectacular.

Cedar bathroom building

Beachwood bathroom building near site 221

Pines bathroom building near site 16

Beachwood bathroom building near site 268

Pines bathroom building near site 50

Beachwood bathroom building near site 337

111

Cell Service

I got one to two bars of service. It's enough to make phone calls and texts, but not great if you want to surf the web.

Beach and Boating

With two gorgeous sandy beaches to choose from, Ludington S.P. is a perfect destination for those that love to lay out in the sun. Hamlin Lake is the inland lake on the east side of the park and is a great place to enjoy the calm relaxing water. It also has a nice playscape for the kids to play on to burn off some energy.

The Lake Michigan beach is a large sandy beach capable of handling a large number of beachgoers on a hot summer day. The recently renovated historic beach house provides the perfect place to change into a swimsuit and or take a break from the sun.

A boat Launch near the beach on Hamlin Lake will accommodate boats up to 20 feet long and a parking lot with trailer parking is available. There is not a boat launch in Lake Michigan in the park and you can not access Lake Michigan from Hamlin Lake because of the dam.

Hamlin Lake beach

Hamlin Lake beach house

Lake Michigan beach house

Lake Michigan beach

Shopping and Restaurants

The park has a small camp store located in the Cedar Campground. It has some basic necessities along with t-shirts and souvenirs. Ludington is about 8 miles away and has about anything you may need, from local gift shops to a Walmart and Home Depot. Ludington also has a plethora of restaurants and bars that are appealing to any taste.

Boardwalk on Hamlin Lake shoreline

Hamlin Lake beach playscape

Park Store in Cedar Campground

Big Sable Lighthouse

Things To Do

With over 5000 acres, a lighthouse, and two lakes, you will not run out of things to do in the park. With over 20 miles of hiking trails, any nature lover will be in heaven. With wetlands and dunes, birders will have opportunities to see plenty of birds. The Big Sable Lighthouse at the northern end of the park is a historic landmark that is a must see when visiting. A 4 mile canoe trail is perfect for paddling around on a warm summer day, either by canoe or kayak.

The Ludington area offers golfing, museums, fishing and a variety of shops and tourist activities to delight any Michigander. You can watch the historic S.S. Badger come in and out of the harbor as it sails across Lake Michigan, to and from Wisconsin. I am sure you will have no problem finding something to do if you want to get away from the park, but with all Ludington S.P. has to offer it will be hard to leave.

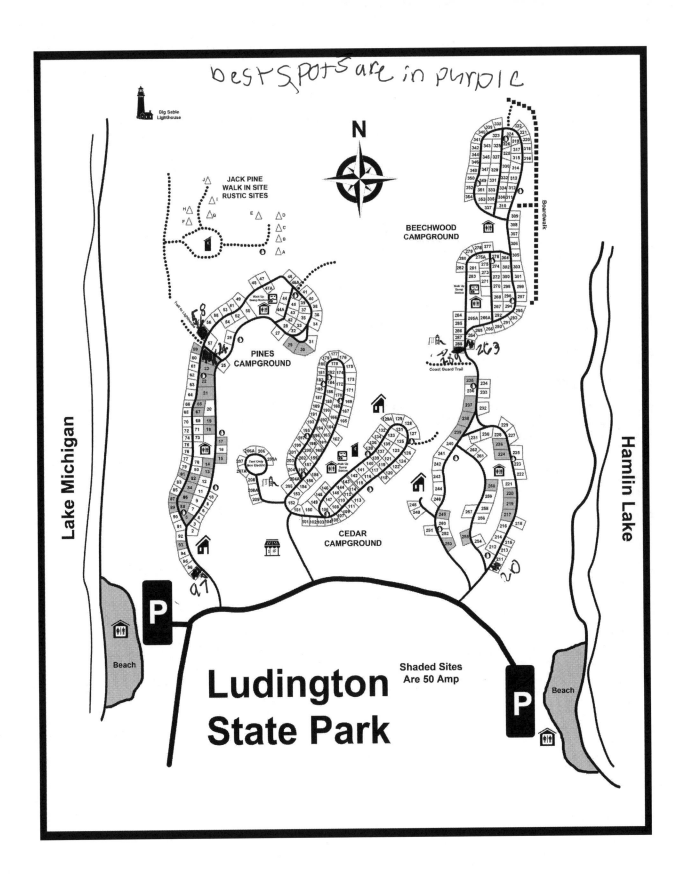

Mears State Park

400 West Lowell Street
Pentwater MI, 49449
231-869-2051

175 campsites
1 cabin
50 acres

Modern opens beginning of April

Modern closes end of October

Semi modern not available

Mears State Park is located near Pentwater, where the Pentwater River empties into Lake Michigan. It is an extremely popular destination with a beautiful sandy beach and is within walking distance to the tourist welcoming town of Pentwater.

Pros
- Next to Pentwater
- Beautiful Lake Michigan beach
- Plenty of tourist activities

Cons
- Small campsites
- One bathroom
- Difficult to get reservations

Campground

The campground at Mears State Park is one of the more unique campgrounds because it is all pavement. It shares that distinction with Grand Haven State Park. I think Mears is a little better designed than Grand Haven because the sites are a little larger but by no means are they large sites. If you have a large trailer, expect to get your trailer and your tow vehicle to fit on your lot and that is about it. You will not have room for a second vehicle. There is a little bit of loose beach sand with a picnic table and fire pit between the sites. The sites towards the south east part of the campground has a few trees for some shade. Expect the rest of the campground to have a lot of sun. If you don't have a large awning on your RV, I would recommend a pop up canopy for some shade.

The sites around the outer edge allows more space except for the sites near site 25. There is a retaining wall that limits the depth of the sites, making it difficult to back your trailer in far from the road.

Reservations

Mears is an extremely popular park and if you want to get a reservation, you will need to try to get them six months to the day. You will need to do this first thing in the morning when the reservation system opens for the day. If you do manage to get a reservation, consider yourself lucky as they are very difficult to obtain during the summer months.

Campground retaining wall

Mears campground

116

Bathrooms

There is only one bathroom building. It is a newer brick building but it does see a lot of use since the campground is always full to capacity. The building has a limited number of showers so you can expect to wait in line for a shower and I would recommend trying to shower at a slower time of day instead of in the morning or evening when most people take showers.

Cell Service

Cell service was O.K. with a couple of bars. The park has WiFi. In my experience, the WiFi connection in campgrounds is slow since it can not handle the hundreds of people connecting to it.

Campground bathroom building

Beach and Boating

The park does not have a boat launch but it does have a large sandy beach on Lake Michigan. It also has a beach house for you to change into your swimsuit.

Beach house at the Lake Michigan beach

Shopping and restaurants

The park does not have a store, but the town of Pentwater is only about 5 blocks away or about ¼ mile. Across from the harbor is a party slash grocery store for most of your basic needs. A few miles away where US-31 exits to Business 31, you will find a couple of gas stations and a Dollar General. If you want to go to a big store, like Meijer, Ludington is about 20 miles to the north.

Things To Do

Besides soaking up some sun on the beach, Mears State Park has a short hiking trail that takes you up Old Baldy, a sand dune with a view of the lake and surrounding area. The beach has a nice playscape for the kids to climb on while you are relaxing in the sand. It's a short trip to Pentwater for gift shops, bars, restaurants and some ice cream shops to enjoy on a hot summer day. You will also find your usual tourist spots like go karts and miniature golf. If you want to explore the dunes of Silver Lake are not far away.

Playscape at the Lake Michigan beach

118

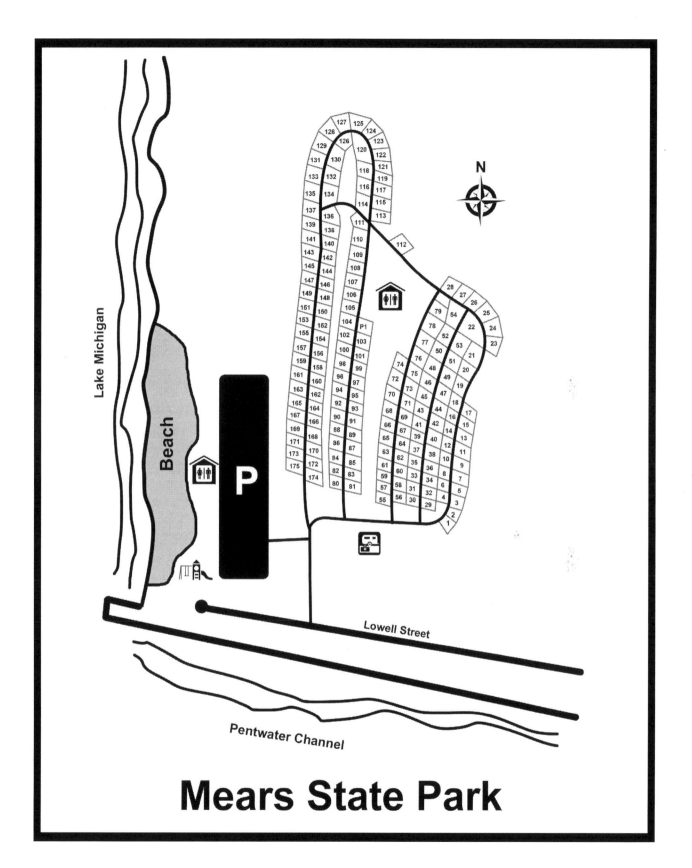

Mears State Park

Harrisville State Park

248 State Park Road
Harrisville MI, 48740
989-724-5126

195 campsites
2 cabins
107 acres

Semi modern open all year

Modern opens mid April

Modern closes end of October

Created in 1921, Harrisville State Park is one of the oldest parks in the state and is one of the more popular parks in the mitten. Not far from the town of Harrisville and nestled along the sandy shores of Lake Huron, it has one of the nicest bathrooms in all of the state parks. It's shoreline campsites are some of the most popular places to stay in the state.

Pros
- New bathroom
- Shoreline campsites
- Near Harrisville

Cons
- Long drive from southern Michigan
- Only one bathroom

Campground

Harrisville is one large campground with 195 campsites. The whole campground is heavily wooded with tall trees that provides plenty of shade. The sites can be a little unlevel but not too bad, but make sure you have leveling boards for your wheels. There is only one bathroom and it is located near the beach. It can be a long walk to the bathroom if you are on the sites farthest from it. The sites near the water are some of the most coveted sites in Michigan. They are a few feet from the lake with a short pathway that leads to a nice sandy beach.

Waterfront campsite

Harrisville campground

Reservations

Harrisville is one of the more popular state parks on the sunrise side of the state and you will want to make reservations early. If you want a lakeside site, you will need to try six months to the day and if you are lucky maybe you will snag one before someone else does.

Bathrooms

The campground has only one bathroom, but it is brand new and probably the best bathroom in all the state park system. Another bathroom is located in the day use area and is an option if you are camping at the south end of the park.

Day use bathroom

Dish washing station at campground bathroom

Campground bathroom

Cell Service

I got a couple of bars of cell signal. It was not as strong as I thought it would be considering the park is in the town of Harrisville, but it is acceptable and should be reliable.

Campground beach on Lake Huron

Day use beach and playground

Beach and Boating

The beach runs along the whole length of the park. The designated swimming areas are next to the bathroom building in the campground and also at the day use in the southern end of the park. It's a nice sandy beach on Lake Huron and probably one of the nicest beaches on the east side of the state.

There is a dog beach at the far northern end of the park if you want to take mans best friend for a swim to cool off on a hot summer day.

The park has a small boat launch. It does not have a dock or cement pad. It's intended for canoes, kayaks, and small rowboats. If you want to launch a bigger boat you will need to go to the state harbor in Harrisville.

Shopping and Restaurants

Harrisville is not a large town, but it is only a mile away and has a small grocery store and some bars and restaurants if you want to take a break from cooking while on vacation. Almost across the street from the entrance to the park is an ice cream shop and some convenience stores. Harrisville also has a Family Dollar and an Ace Hardware. If you need to go to a big city, Alpena is about 30 miles north of the park on M-23.

Things To Do

The park has a couple of miles of hiking trails to explore or you could go to nearby Negwegon State Park if hiking is your thing. Sturgeon Point Lighthouse is not far away and the grounds are open to visitors all summer long. Alpena is a great town to explore, and is home to the Great Lakes Maritime Heritage Center.

123

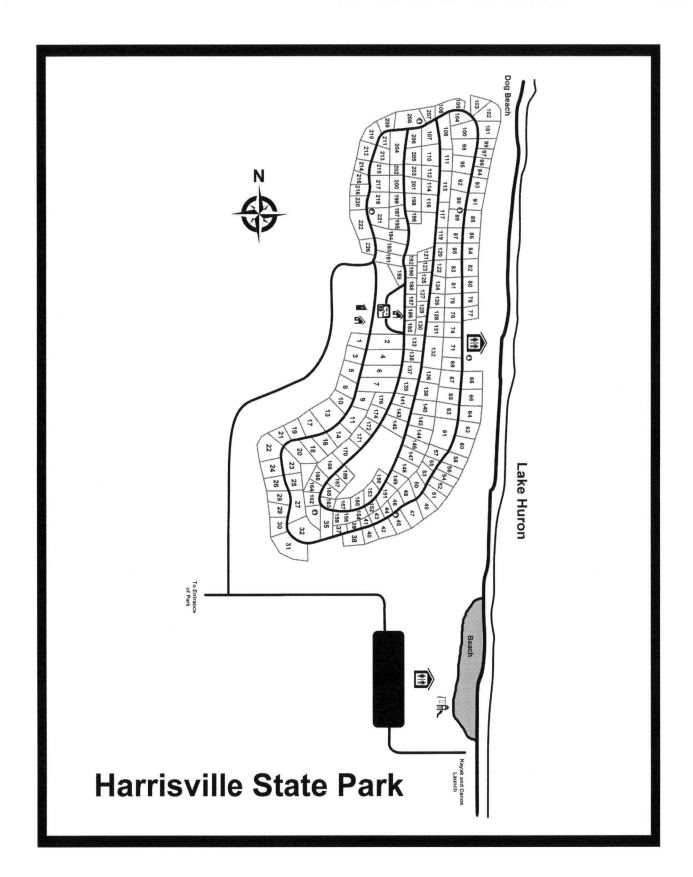

Harrisville State Park

Tawas Point State Park

686 Tawas Beach Road
East Tawas MI, 48730
989-362-5041

193 campsites
4 cabins
1 yurt
183 acres

Modern camping available all year

Tawas Point State Park is one of the most popular parks in the Michigan State Park system and probably the most popular park in the east side of the state. If you want to camp here in the summer you definitely need to make reservations six months to the day. The park sits on the tip of a point that sticks out into Lake Huron. Some refer to it as the "Cape Cod of Michigan"

Pros
- Near East Tawas
- Beautiful Beaches
- Nice Bathroom Buildings

Cons
- Popular park and can be difficult to get reservations
- Sites are small

Campground

The campground has 193 campsites and there are only a few trees so the sites are mostly open and sunny. In my opinion, the sites seem to be smaller than they are in other state parks that I have camped at. It's a beautiful place to camp on a point into Lake Huron, away from any busy roads. Just be aware that in the summer the park is usually full, even midweek, so there will be a lot of people in the campground. The sites to the south are near the water along Tawas Bay and are the most popular sites in the park. There are some trees between the water and the campsite, so you probably won't be able to look out over the water while sitting at your campsite. The campground is flat so no matter where your site is it will be relatively level. I don't have a large trailer, but if you do, be prepared for the streets in the campground to be tight. It can be tricky to back into your site. Be sure to have a spotter or a couple of spotters to help with backing up.

Tawas Point campground

Reservations

Tawas Point SP is one of the more popular parks and if you want to camp here, you need to make reservations six months to the day. The lots closest to the bay are taken first so be sure to try for those when the system lets you reserve them at 8 am.

Bathrooms

The campground has two identical modern bathrooms. They are newer bathrooms that seem to be well maintained. They also have a dishwashing station for washing out pots and pans after cooking dinner which is really helpful if you are camping in a tent.

One of two identical campground bathrooms

Dishwashing station

126

Beach and Boating

There are two beaches in the state park. The main beach is over by the lighthouse along Lake Huron and has a large bathhouse. The other beach is on Tawas Bay in the campground. Both are wonderful beaches, but the size of the beach varies depending on the water level of Lake Huron. A few years ago, the water level was low and there was plenty of sand before you got to the waterline. In recent years water levels are high so the beaches are smaller than usual, but still worth going to. I know many people who say they are the nicest beaches on Lake Huron. If you go camping with mans best friend, there is also a dog beach to take them swimming on hot summer days.

Cell Service

The signal is not strong, but it is enough to make calls, text and surf the web a little.

Campground beach

Lake Huron day use beach

127

Shopping and restaurants

The Park is about 5 miles from downtown East Tawas. Just to clarify, there are two cities next to each other Tawas and East Tawas (which is north of Tawas, I did not come up with the names). The main tourist district is located near the harbor in East Tawas. I think it is one of the reasons why the park is so popular, since there are a variety of shops and restaurants to visit. Tawas is a large enough town to have anything you may need with a Walmart and hardware stores. If you need something, it's not a long drive to get it.

Tawas Point Lighthouse

Things to Do

The best thing to do at Tawas Point S.P. is the historic lighthouse. Even if you are not camping and you have never been to the State Park it's worth the trip just to see the lighthouse, which is open for tours on the weekends. There are hiking trails through the marshlands of the park which is popular with birders. In May, a variety of bird species migrate through the parks. If you are working on a "big year" or just enjoy watching birds, the park is a good place to visit. Lumbermans Monument and Iargo Springs along the Ausable River is about 20 miles away. It makes for a nice road trip if you want to go exploring.

Playground at Lake Huron day use beach

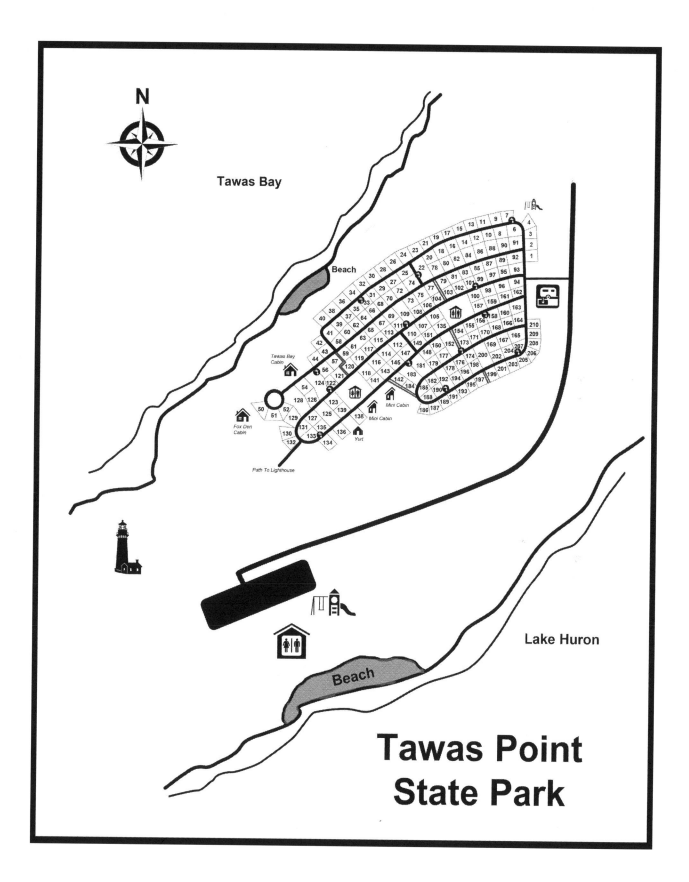

Tawas Bay

Beach

Tawas Bay Cabin

Fox Den Cabin

Path To Lighthouse

Mini Cabin

Mini Cabin

Yurt

Lake Huron

Beach

Tawas Point
State Park

Rifle River Recreation Area

2550 E. Rose City Road
Lupton MI, 48635-0098
989-473-2258

75 modern campsites
99 rustic campsites
5 cabins
4449 acres

Modern campsites and bathroom
open all year

Rifle River Recreation Area is an outdoor lovers paradise, and is one of the largest parks in the system with 4445 acres. With its miles of hiking trails, 5 lakes that do not allow motors and the Rifle River flowing through the park it is the perfect place to experience nature.

Pros
- Large park with an abundance of activities for nature lovers.
- Near the center of the state
- Rifle River flows through the park

Cons
- Limited number of modern campsites
- Far away from shopping

Campgrounds

The park has four different campgrounds.

Grousehaven

Grousehaven Campground has modern sites with electricity and a bathroom building with flush toilets and showers. There are two different loops, a north loop which has more trees and shade and a south loop which has almost no trees and is full sun. The bathroom building is between them so no matter which loop you are in, you will use the same bathroom. The beach is next to the bathroom but is easier to access from the south loop. It's a nice beach even though it's not a large beach which is OK since there are not many sites in Grousehaven. There is a separate beach on the other side of the lake for day use.

Grousehaven north campground

Devoe

Devoe Campground is a rustic campground about 2 miles into the park, next to Devoe Lake. The campground does not have any sites on the water, and all of the sites are wooded with plenty of trees and shade. Since it's rustic there is no electricity with pit toilets and a hand pump for water. The sites are spread out, and more secluded than the modern campground. The beach on Devoe Lake is nice and sandy and has some grassy areas with picnic tables. It's a little bit of a walk from the campsites to the beach. About a 200 to 500 yards depending on what campsite you are staying at.

Ranch and Spruce

Ranch and Spruce Campgrounds are about 3 miles from the entrance of the park. Both are rustic and on the Rifle River. There are a few campsites that are right next to the river. Both campgrounds are wooded with shade and have pit toilets and hand pumps for water.

Grousehaven south campground

Reservations

For reservations at Grousehaven I would recommend making them six months to the day for any date between Memorial Day to Labor Day. The campsites go quickly since there are only 80 of them in the modern campground. It is usually easier to get a site at the rustic campgrounds. I have seen sites available a week before the big 4th of July holiday.

Bathrooms

The only campground with a modern bathroom is Grousehaven. It is a brick building with showers along the end hallway. It is a nice building and well maintained. The other campgrounds are rustic and only have pit toilets.

Beaches and Boating

Besides the beaches at Grousehaven and Devoe Campgrounds the park has a day use beach on the Northeast side of Grousehaven Lake. It is a nice sandy beach with a large grassy area for picnicking. Tables and grills are available for visitors to use.

The lakes in the Rifle River Recreation Area are "no motor" lakes and boats can not have motors on them. Grebe lake has am ADA accessible kayak and canoe launch.

Cell Service

Cell service was not strong in the campgrounds but I did get a signal. It Is a large park and there may be places where you will not get a signal when you are on the hiking trails.

Grousehaven campground bathroom building

Grousehaven campground beach

Shopping and Restaurants

The nearest store to the park is a convenience store across from the entrance. Remember, even though it's near the entrance you still have about a 3 mile drive on a rough dirt road to get to the store from the rustic campgrounds in the back of the park. It is a nice store with a good selection of snacks and basic needs. Most importantly they have ice cream for those hot summer days. I love the ice cave. They must sell a lot of ice to rustic campers for coolers. The nearest grocery store is in Rose city about 9 miles away. They also have a McDonald's, Subway and Dairy Queen if you don't want to cook. If you want to do some serious shopping downtown Tawas is about a half hour drive.

Things to do

Rifle River Recreation Area is the perfect place to get out and enjoy Nature. Hiking the miles of trails or paddling down the Rifle River are some of the most popular activities. The park has several lakes which are motor free and allow for a quiet time of fishing or just floating around and relaxing. The convenience store across from the campground rents canoes and kayaks. On hot summer days you can cool off by swimming at one of the beaches in the park. If you want to get out of the park and explore Lumberman's Monument is about 25 miles away.

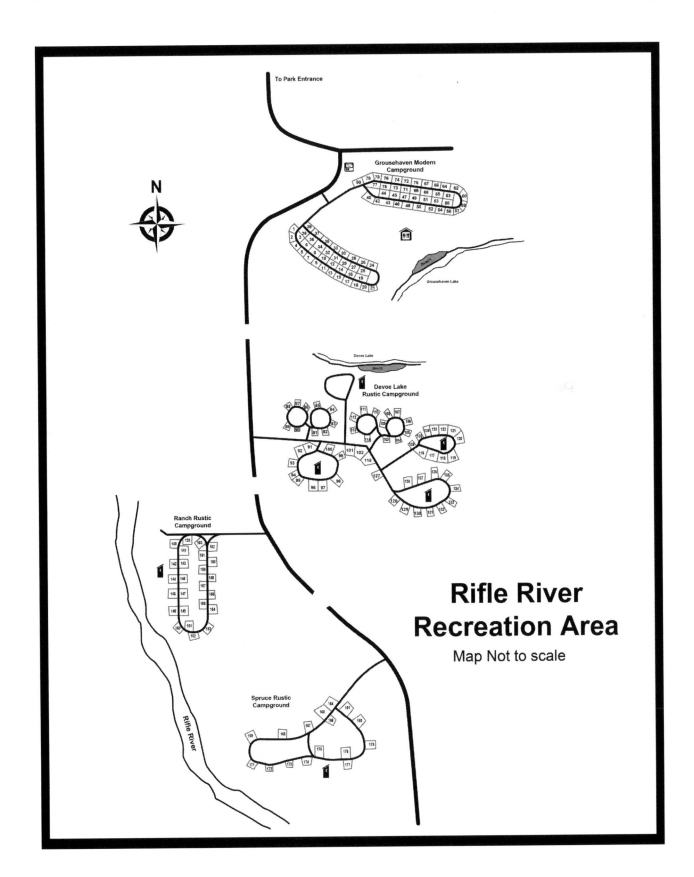

**Rifle River
Recreation Area**

Map Not to scale

Bay City Recreation Area

3582 State Park Dr.
Bay City MI, 48706-1356
(989) 684-3020

193 campsites
2 mini cabins
2000 acres

Modern opens late April

Modern closes late October

Semi Modern open all year

If you love to hike and go antiquing, Bay City State Recreation Area is a park you should stay at. North of beautiful Bay City, on the Saginaw Bay, the park contains Tobico Marsh with miles of trails for outdoor enthusiasts. Downtown Bay City with its large antique shops and unique specialty stores is a few miles away.

Pros

- Excellent place for hiking and birding
- Not a long drive from Metro Detroit and other cities
- Near downtown Bay City
- Newer bathroom facilities
- Playscape and splash park

Cons

- Beach can be mucky at times or even closed
- No campsites overlooking the bay
- You have to cross the road to get to the beach
- No boat launch in the park

Campground

For the most part, the campground is flat and the sites are level. It's also wooded and the sites are shaded except for the sites nearest the entrance which have fewer trees and can be full sun. The campground is laid out perpendicular from the beach that is across the road from the park. The sites closest to the entrance are closest to the beach. If you are in the back of the campground it's a long walk to the beach. The sites in the back of the park are near the road and they can be a little noisy.

Reservations

Reservations at the campground are usually easy to get as it's not one of the most popular parks in the system for camping. As always, you should book as early as you can for holiday weekends. I did manage to get a site a few weeks before Labor Day. I rechecked a few days before the holiday and it was full. If you are going to camp in October, be sure to book early since the park's Harvest Festival is extremely popular.

Bathrooms

The bathrooms at the park are both newer identical bathroom buildings, so if you like to be near the bathroom either one would be good. They are what I call the typical design, with a walkway with a row of showers on one side and the men's and women's bathrooms on the other. They seem to be well maintained.

Two identical bathroom buildings

Bay City campground

Cell Service

I had about 3 bars of service while in Bay City R.A. Located near Bay City I would expect to get some sort of cell service.

Beach

The beach is a nice large beach on the Saginaw Bay. The staff does their best to maintain the beach but it's kind of a hit or miss thing. Being near wetlands and marshes, the water along the edge of the beach can get mucky. It's rare but the biggest issue is that the beach has been closed a few times in the summer due to high levels of E-coli. If swimming is a high priority you may not like Bay City S.R.A. They do have a large playscape and splash park. I wonder if they built them because of the beach closures.

Splash park in day use area

Fishing dock

Playscape in day use area

Shopping and Restaurants

If you need groceries, there are a couple of party stores a few miles south of the park. Walmart, Home Depot or just about everything else are about 7 miles south of the campground. If you don't feel like cooking Mussel Beach restaurant is right around the corner. I have not eaten there but several people tell me it's good. They also serve ice cream if you're looking for a cool treat to end a hot summer day. With some of the largest antique stores in Michigan, downtown Bay City is the perfect place to shop for the exotic one of a kind item. Downtown has a lot of bars, restaurants and gift shops. You could easily spend an afternoon or even a whole day wandering around all the stores.

Things To Do

The best part of Bay City R.A. is Tobico Marsh, north of the campground on the other side of the road. It has miles of trails through forests and wetlands that are sure to make any nature lover happy. I am not a birder, but if you are going for a big year there should be a lot of different species to spot in the wetlands. A paved rail trail that runs behind the campground goes for miles north through Tobico Marsh. I rode my bike down it with the intention of reaching the end but after a long ride, I became tired and turned around before I could find the end, if there is one. I am sure a devoted cyclist who is in better shape than me would enjoy riding their bicycle through the marsh. In August, the park has a Waterfowl Festival and in October a Harvest Festival. The Bay City Recreation Area is also home to the Saginaw Bay Visitor Center with nature-based activities and programs for kids of all ages

Tobico Marsh hiking trails

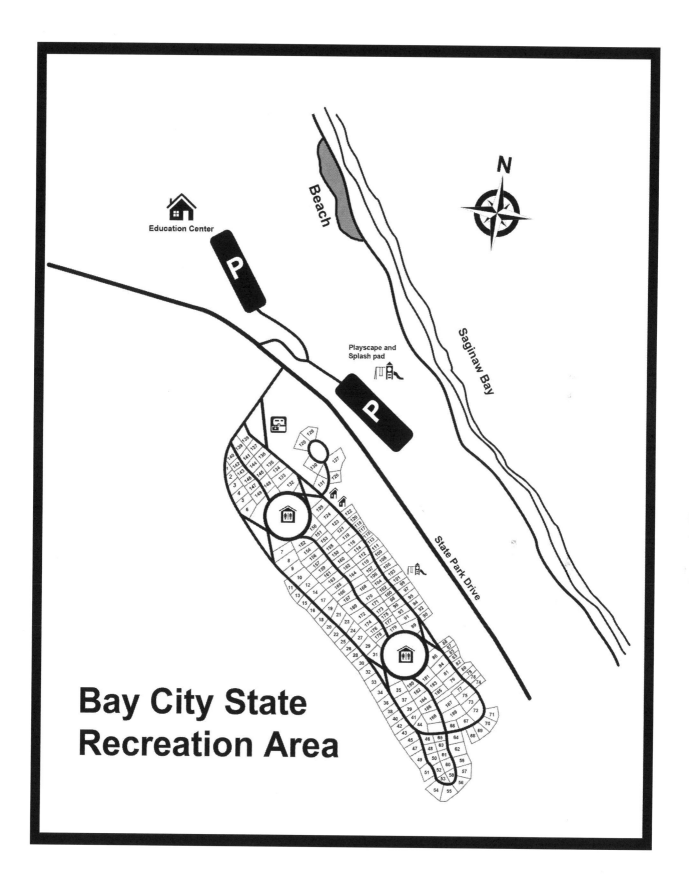

Bay City State
Recreation Area

Sleeper State Park

6573 State Park Road
Caseville MI, 48725-9799
989-856-4411

226 campsites
1 mini cabin
723 acres

Modern and semi modern
opens mid April

Modern closes mid October

Semi modern closes
end of November

Located along the Saginaw Bay in Michigan's Thumb, Sleeper State Park is an excellent place to kick back and relax. Only a few miles north east of Caseville, it is a popular place to stay during the town's many festivals including the Cheeseburger in Caseville Festival. The park first opened as a county park in 1925 and the state took over in 1927. The name was changed to Sleeper State Park in 1944 in honor of Governor Albert Sleeper, who signed the law that created the state park system in Michigan.

Pros
- Large campground with a large number of sites
- Some sites can accommodate large RVs
- Near Caseville

Cons
- Next to M-25
- Beach is on other side of road from campground

Campground

The campground has 226 campsites and is divided into a west and an east section.

The west section is the more popular of the two. It has a newer bathroom along with larger sites. The sites tend to be more level and grassy compared to the east side where the sites are smaller and not as level.

M-25 runs along the north side of the campground. The sites are about 50 to 100 feet from the road with trees separating it for a little privacy. In general, the sites nearest M-25 tend to be more grassy and open. Further away from the road the sites tend to be more wooded and unlevel. The sites in the back row are small, with mounds around the trees and it can be difficult to get a trailer on them, especially a large trailer.

Reservations

The park is popular since it is one of only two state parks near the tip of the thumb. Port Crescent in Port Austin is more popular of the two, making it is a little easier to get reservations for Sleeper State Park. For holiday weekends and the famous Cheeseburger in Caseville Festival you will want to make your reservations six months to the day. You should be able to reserve a site for the summertime if you make reservations in early spring.

West campground

East campground

141

Bathrooms

The west side of the campground has a new brick bathroom building. It is the common style of bathroom, with showers on one side of a hallway and bathrooms on the other. The east side has an older bathroom. It's an OK bathroom, but the newer one on the west side is preferred.

Cell Service

I had two bars of cell service. Being near Caseville, you should be able to get some sort of signal but probably not a really strong one.

East bathroom building

West bathroom building

Beach and Boating

The beach at Sleeper is a large sandy beach that stretches for about a half mile along the Saginaw Bay. Unfortunately, it's on the other side of M-25. There is a walkway that goes up and over the busy state highway but it makes for a long walk to the beach.

Sleeper State Park does not have a boat launch. Nearby Caseville has a marina where you can launch a boat.

Beach on Saginaw Bay

Shopping and Restaurants

There is a party store on M-25, just east of the campground. If you need something more than what you can find at a party store, Caseville is about 5 miles away on M-25. Caseville has some local restaurants and bars if you don't feel like cooking. If you want to get fast food or go to a big box store like Walmart, the nearest "big city" is Bad Axe, which is about 25 miles away.

Things To Do

Besides laying out in the sun on the beach the state park has about 700 acres of wilderness to explore and over 4 miles of hiking trails to hike. Both Caseville and nearby Port Austin provide a chance to gift shop and play miniature golf. You could rent a kayak in Port Austin and paddle out to the famous Turnip Rock which is only accessible by boat.

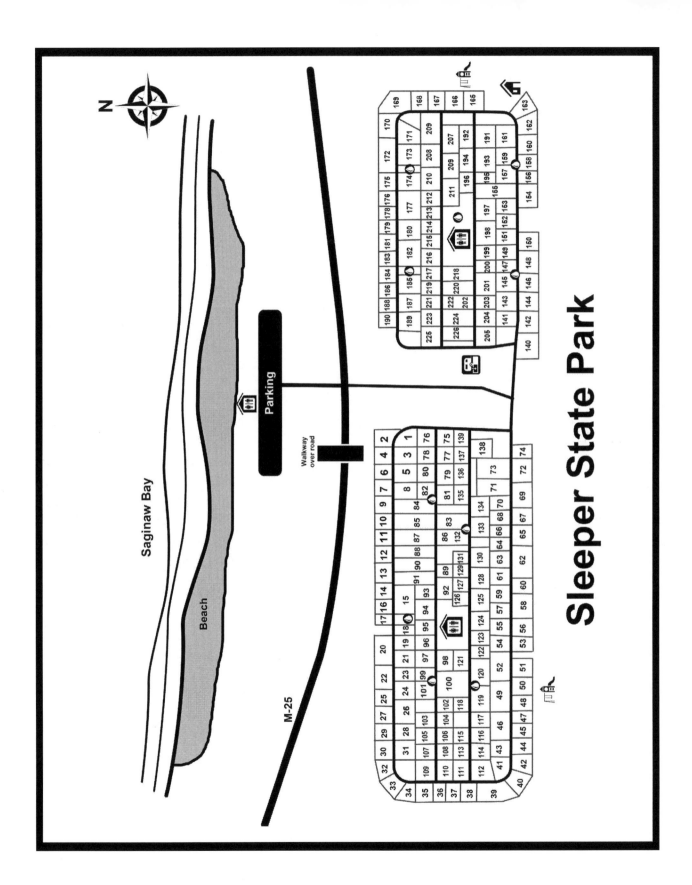

Sleeper State Park

Port Crescent State Park

1775 Port Austin Road
Port Austin MI, 48467
989-738-8663

142 campsites
2 cabins
640 acres

Modern open mid April

Modern closes end of October

No semi modern available

Port Crescent State Park is on the Saginaw Bay about 6 miles south west of Port Austin. It's a large park with sand dunes to hike and explore and the sites located on the water are extremely popular. If you are looking for a place to stay while you explore the tip of the Thumb, Port Crescent State Park is one of the best places for camping along the Saginaw Bay.

Pros
- Sandy Shoreline
- Large park to hike and explore
- Waterfront sites

Cons
- Sites are small
- Sites can be sandy

Campground

The campground has a 142 sites with electric hookup. It stretches along the Saginaw Bay shoreline with several sites right on the water. The park is rather hilly with sites that either cut into the hill or have steep drop offs behind them. Many of the sites are not deep, making it difficult to fit a large trailer on them. If you make reservations, be sure to look at the site dimensions to be sure your trailer will fit. The sites towards the beach tend to be rather sandy and some only have an asphalt pad surrounded by sand. The park is wooded throughout with very few sites with full sun. The most requested sites are the ones right next to the water and the sandy beach that runs along the shore. Note that there are public pathways for other campers to have access to the water and you will have people walking along the shore next to your campsite. The campground is off M-25 and sites around site 44 are close to the road. A fence separates the campground from the road, but you will hear cars passing by.

Reservations

Port Crescent is a popular park for those wanting to stay in Michigan's thumb. You are going to want to make reservations as soon as you can. To get the coveted waterfront sites, you will need to make reservations six months to the day and even then you will be lucky to get one. You will also want to make reservations six months to the day for holiday weekends.

Port Crescent campsite

Campsite near the shoreline

Bathrooms

The park has two bathrooms. The bathroom at the northeast end of the park, farthest from the entrance, is a newer facility. The bathroom near the beach and playground is an older bathroom but is maintained well.

Cell Service

I had 2 bars of cell service when I was there. With Port Austin not far away from the park you should get acceptable cell service.

Bathroom building near the entrance

Bathroom near the east end of the campground

147

Beach and Boating

The campground has a nice sandy beach but it seems a little small for the number of campsites so it can be crowded during hot busy weekends. The beach is towards the entrance of the park, so if you are on a site near the back of the park, it can be a long walk. There are access paths to the water between some of the sites along the shoreline.

The park does not have a boat launch, but there is a harbor in nearby Port Austin.

Shopping and Restaurants

The park does not have a camp store but there is a party store directly across the street from the entrance. Port Austin is about six miles away and has an IGA grocery store along with gift shops and restaurants. If you need to go to a big box store, Bad Axe is about 20 miles away.

Things To Do

The park has 7 miles of hiking trails on 640 acres of land. The Pinnebog River meanders through the center of the park with fishing docks and access sites for kayakers. Nearby Port Austin has miniature golf and kayak rental for those wanting to paddle out to Turnip Rock. You're not far from Grindstone City, and the general store in this town is known for their home made ice cream with gigantic ice cream cones.

Playground near the beach

Beach on Saginaw Bay

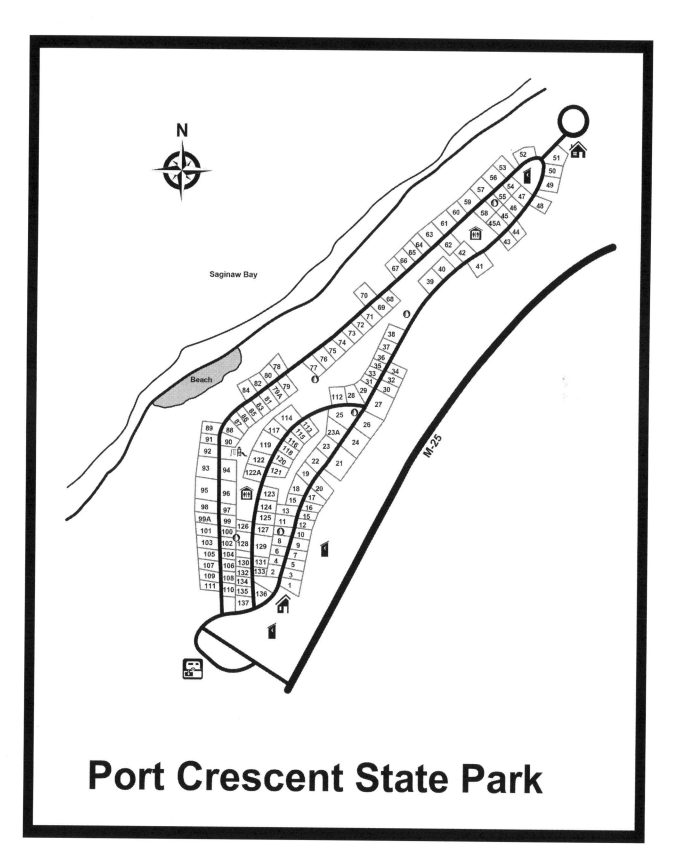

Port Crescent State Park

About the Author

Mike Sonnenberg was born and raised in Saginaw Michigan where he currently resides. He worked in the automotive industry designing test and assembly machines for about 20 years. Starting in 2013 he began traveling the back roads of Michigan in search of forgotten or overlooked places. He created the Lost In Michigan website posting photos and stories of the interesting places he has found. Sonnenberg's work has been featured in the Detroit Free Press and he is considered a "Michigan Expert" by USA Today. In the fall of 2017, he published two books based on the posts on his website. He still continues to travel around Michigan looking for unique places to tell their story. You can follow his journey at www.LostinMichigan.net

**For more campground reviews
or to order books visit**

www.CampMichigan.org

Made in the USA
Lexington, KY
13 June 2019